Cynthia Heald has long been a trusted author of
Bible studies, books, and devotionals designed to help
women know and follow Jesus. In *Living Wisely*, she
encourages women to experience blessed, fruitful lives
through embracing the timeless wisdom of his Word.
Women in every season will find this book helpful, but
I am especially hopeful that younger women will take
advantage of the opportunity to learn these vital truths
from a wise, older woman. They will thank me one day,
when they are "older women" themselves!

NANCY DeMOSS WOLGEMUTH, author, Bible teacher, and
founder of Revive Our Hearts

In *Living Wisely*, Cynthia shows how God and his Word
not only speak to but can deeply transform us as we face
the impending realities of life. This book is for every person
who wants to live a life of freedom and deep peace as they
walk through any possible occurrence in life. *Living Wisely*
is a book every disciple should embrace as well as pass on to
those they are helping grow.

DANA YEAKLEY, author of *The Gentle Art of Discipling Women*

Cynthia Heald encourages us to travel the narrow road with
Christ and shows us how to "hold on to his hand when the
way [is] dark." In her keen exploration of biblical truths,
we learn that a life freed of self and abandoned to God is
the true pathway to abundant life.

BEKAH DiFELIC

Cynthia's Bible studies and writing have shaped my life for years. In *Living Wisely*, she again combines the stories of real people in real-life challenges with life-changing, true, and real words of wisdom from the Scriptures. This study invites us to new places of surrender and trust in our unchangeable and good God. Cynthia masterfully points us to the real source of love and life! As she emphasizes on every page, remember—"keep your hand in his."

**LINDY BLACK,** associate US director of The Navigators

Cynthia is a gentle guide, showing us how to walk the "narrow way" with her wisdom, experience, and grace. She has learned from the Master how to walk in true freedom, and I'm grateful for her heart to lead us to his feet.

**JESSIE MINASSIAN,** author of *Unashamed*

I love this book. Its fragrance is captivating, and it drew me in to the truths shared throughout these pages. Cynthia validates the relevance and veracity of God's truth by telling her story and the stories of others and by punctuating each with biblical truth. In our present culture, where there are no absolutes and no road map, *Living Wisely* shows us that his absolute truth is the only map we need to navigate through to real life. *Living Wisely* is timeless and has a message of wisdom and guidance for all generations. Not only will I be sharing Cynthia's book with many others, it is a keeper and will be taken from my own bookshelf many times as I seek guidance and wisdom.

**DR. CYNTHIA FANTASIA,** former pastor of women at Grace Chapel, author of *In the Lingering Light*

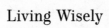

Living Wisely

A NavPress resource published in alliance
with Tyndale House Publishers

CYNTHIA HEALD

# Living Wisely

BELIEVING THE TRUTHS OF SCRIPTURE

NavPress is the publishing ministry of The Navigators, an international Christian organization and leader in personal spiritual development. NavPress is committed to helping people grow spiritually and enjoy lives of meaning and hope through personal and group resources that are biblically rooted, culturally relevant, and highly practical.

**For more information, visit www.NavPress.com.**

*To my mentor, Mary Tabb, who lovingly
and patiently prepared me to walk the
narrow way and to want to live wisely.*

# Contents

Author's Note  *xi*

Introduction: My Search for Wisdom  *1*

1. Maybe God Is Right After All  *15*
2. God Is for You, Not against You  *29*
3. Trust God, Even When It Doesn't Make Sense  *43*
4. Freedom from Self Is a Choice  *59*
5. Keep Your Hand in His  *75*
6. God's Word Is All the Truth You'll Ever Need  *91*
7. You Will Never Regret Doing What Is Right  *107*
8. Love Is Not Optional  *121*
9. Forgiveness Frees the Forgiver  *137*
10. It's God's Life  *153*

A Final Word: The Best Is Yet to Come  *167*

Notes  *181*

About the Author  *189*

# Author's Note

*Thank you for wanting to read this book. I am honored to be a small part of your life as you consider the truths that continue to transform my life.*

*You can use this book in several ways. As I have written it, I have pictured myself sitting across the table from you and sharing my heart as we have a cup of tea. I have tried to anticipate your questions and needs. Enjoy the book as a kind of conversation between the two of us.*

*You can also use the book in a group Bible study or book club. After each chapter, you will find reflection questions and Bible verses that can help stimulate discussion about what you have read.*

*I pray that, however you read and study this book, you will desire in a fresh way to grow in wisdom so you may live wisely in our perplexing world. "Wisdom is far more valuable than rubies. Nothing you desire can compare with it."[1]*

*Blessings as you take hold of his hand and walk in his true and right paths.*

*Cynthia Heald*

INTRODUCTION

# MY SEARCH FOR WISDOM

*Two roads diverged in a wood, and I—*
*I took the one less traveled by,*
*And that has made all the difference.*

ROBERT FROST, "The Road Not Taken"


*Getting wisdom is the wisest thing you can do!*
*And whatever else you do, develop good judgment.*
*If you prize wisdom, she will make you great.*
*Embrace her, and she will honor you.*

PROVERBS 4:7-8

IT WAS SEPTEMBER 1959. The "Psychedelic Sixties" were about to explode into a countercultural movement that would have an impact on our country for decades. I was a twenty-year-old senior on a university campus, and three of my friends and I were moving into a large, off-campus house that had been remodeled for a semi-communal living project. The directors of this venture had a vision for teaching qualified students to think philosophically, to be exposed to the basic tenets of world religions, and to learn about how to live together in a true community.

This unique opportunity was a radical concept for our university campus: an atmosphere of intellectual exploration of truth with others who were committed to the same goals. And it was just what I was looking for. My teen years were spent in the conservative 1950s, but in college, I began to read and listen to the voices that called for revolutionary ideas. This new community seemed to provide a perfect, safe place to examine truth and learn how to make a difference in the world. I was in the right place at the right time.

Each week, the members of our community attended two night classes. We read numerous authors, such as: Jean-Paul Sartre, Charles Darwin, Søren Kierkegaard, and Rudolf Bultmann. We were intent on exploring a wide spectrum of viewpoints about the significance of life and how we should live in a world of uncertainty.

As part of our community lifestyle, we ate evening meals together and then launched into lively discussions about current issues and world problems, from the Cold War with Russia to the coming free-love revolution. One of the members of our group was in a continual state of distress because he believed that an atomic war with Russia was imminent. Our group was passionate about race relations, and our fervor led us to insist on a meeting with the president of our university. He graciously invited a few of us to lunch and listened to our pleas for racial integration on our campus and in our country. Our group fiercely debated questions about how religion should affect our lives, what the purpose of life is, and our right to challenge the status quo.

Little did I know that we, along with countless other students, were planting the seeds for the coming civil rights movement and the Vietnam War protests. We were the forerunners and future leaders of Students for a Democratic Society (SDS) on our campus. This community was in every way a challenge to "the establishment," and I felt that I was on the cutting edge of our culture, poised to change the world.

But within this community, I had a more personal goal: I was searching for foundational truth to live by. I wanted truth that would anchor my life and give it meaning—truth that would enable me to really live, not just exist. I wanted my life to count; I wanted to make a contribution to the world. I didn't want just to blend in with everyone else and settle into a mundane routine for the rest of my life. I was searching for spiritual truths that would give my life purpose and passion. I wanted to take the road less traveled.

Initially, my involvement in this group of students was

exhilarating. I had never really wrestled with differing philosophies about life, and our studies stretched my mind and challenged my thinking. But as the months wore on, I became discouraged. Nearly all of our study centered on *existentialism*, a twentieth-century philosophical movement "embracing diverse doctrines but centering on analysis of individual existence in an unfathomable universe and the plight of the individual who must assume ultimate responsibility for acts of free will without any certain knowledge of what is right or wrong or good or bad."[1] At first, I found freedom in existentialism and its focus on individualism and self-determination. But as I explored the worldview more closely, I saw lots of ambiguity. I felt increasingly isolated as I thought about my inability to be certain about what was right and wrong. Was it all truly up to me?

The more I encountered ambiguity, the more helpless I felt. Even the great philosophers had no relevant answers for me—and yet I still had to make my way in a world seemingly filled with futility. I remember reading Sartre's play *No Exit*. That title summed up all I was learning. I was adrift in a world without meaning, and what I was studying gave me no signposts to guide me to truth.

I had entered the program to find pivotal truths to live by, but the far-reaching ideas presented in our discussions and seminars all seemed to come to the same conclusion: There are no absolutes, and you have to make your own way in an uncertain world. This pursuit became even more lonely because most of the people in our group were so concerned with their own issues that mutual support was rare. I was disheartened, to say the least.

Was this all the great thinkers had to offer? Were these the definitive answers to life? Where else could I go to find truth? Was anyone else seeking to live like this? Could I find people who were willing to help and serve others, not just a cause? Without realizing it, I breathed a silent prayer: *I want to walk to the beat of a different drummer, but I'd like the drumbeats to communicate hope and a sense of what is true and right.*

I finished out my college years feeling somewhat unfulfilled. Marriage to Jack and teaching quickly followed my graduation and brought contentment, yet I eventually settled into the mundane routine I had so wanted to avoid. I began to think that perhaps life did consist in just making my own way and doing the best I could in the circumstances I was in.

In my more honest moments, however, I still yearned for truth and wisdom, for something I could count on. When Jack and I had moved to a new city, I was still searching when Mary, a newfound friend, invited me to a luncheon, which I was somewhat surprised to discover had a Christian emphasis. As I listened to the speaker, I was captivated by her gentle spirit and her apparent personal relationship with God. I had never heard anyone talk about reading the Bible, understanding it, and applying it to life. So when Mary invited me to a Bible study, I was curious and liked the idea of including this bestseller on my list of study books.

I had a fleeting familiarity with the Bible. I had grown up in a middle-class, churchgoing family. When I was twelve years old, I was marched down to the front of our church and asked if I believed that Jesus Christ was the Son of God. I answered "Yes" and was baptized that night. I was as sincere as a twelve-year-old can be, but the roots of my seedling faith were not cultivated or nurtured. As a result, my faith never grew.

In preparation for Mary's Bible study, I bought a Bible and painstakingly looked up the Scripture verses and recorded the passages' page numbers by each question so I could quickly find the reference when we met as a group. As I began to study the Scriptures and listen to the other women talk about "the Lord" and how the verses helped them in their everyday lives, I was deeply touched.

This was the first time since college that I had met other people who were searching for truth. These women were sincere and convinced that God's Word spoke specifically to their lives for their good. I realized that they were studying not to gain knowledge but to learn truth that would change their lives.

As I observed the interactions and dynamics of this group of women, I was amazed to see that they were really seeking to live in a different kind of way. They wanted their relationship with God to be evident to others. They wanted to be honest and to be held accountable for what they were learning from the Bible. They truly cared about each other, and soon, they cared about me, too. For me, this was a taste of true community.

After a few months of study, I discovered an amazing,

revolutionary truth—the Jesus Christ I met in the Bible was everything I'd been searching for. Jesus modeled radical, wholehearted living as he slipped silently into our world and then boldly proceeded to step on the toes of the religious leaders and philosophers of the time. He taught that true religion—true faith—was based not on rules or philosophical ideas but on a vital, life-changing relationship with the living God. Jesus embodied not only truth and wisdom but also grace and love.

His teaching was unconventional: Love your enemies. Be reconciled to others. Don't call attention to your acts of charity. Forgive those who hurt you. Your treasure is where your heart is. Don't worry about everyday life. Stop judging others. Give, and it will be given to you. Humble yourself, and you will be exalted. Those who cling to life in this world will lose it, but those who surrender their lives will keep them for eternity.[2]

Jesus not only taught profound truth but also sacrificed himself in the ultimate radical act: He voluntarily gave his life so that all who believe in him could know eternal, unerring truth that transforms lives and offers authentic freedom.

I could not help but come to the overwhelming conclusion that Jesus is the Truth. He is the only one who lived, taught, and embodied truth that made sense and felt right. With a heart grateful to God, I realized that I had found the truth for which my heart had been longing—truth that empowered me to live wisely.

I had a burning desire to grow and learn all that I could.

My faith was finally starting to mature. Whenever I visited Mary, I was so eager to learn as much as I could that I would forget the time. She would often be forced to ask me, "Cynthia, would you like to stay for lunch?" Mary and her husband, Don, invited Jack and me to a Bible study for couples. As we experienced the fellowship of these dedicated believers, Jack met Christ personally for the first time.

My search for the truth had ended. I learned that those who believe in Christ and follow him are commissioned to make a difference in the world by living like him. As I learned more about Christ's life, my own life took on meaning and purpose. I found new passion and hope. God's ways are revolutionary, but they are right and wise and good. A life lived with him provides a community that exists to love one another and to give, serve, and minister to those in need.

Over the years, my love for the Scriptures has deepened so much that I now write Bible studies and books about Christian living. I never prayed about or intended to have a writing and speaking ministry, but God's ways are not always our ways. After being challenged by a verse of Scripture found in the book of Ruth, I wrote a Bible-study course entitled "Becoming a Woman of Excellence" and taught it to the women in our church. A friend heard about it and made an appointment for me to talk about the study with an editor. Before long, I began writing Bible studies for publication.

My husband also had a course correction in his life. Jack enjoyed his practice of veterinary medicine for many years, but he gradually felt that God was asking him to trade pets for people, and we now serve on the staff of a worldwide discipleship ministry.

Today, as I look back on several decades of living the life Christ offers, I see that he has revealed several relevant truths that have offered me guidance and wisdom on my journey. These are the rock-bottom truths I return to in life's difficult times or when I find myself at a crossroad and need to make a critical decision.

As I meet with people all across the country, I find that they are searching too. They have questions about the important issues in life. They want their lives to count for something larger than themselves. They want to know how to discern what is right and what is wrong. They want to live wisely—and I find that my responses usually include one or two of ten truths that have become foundational in my life.

I share these truths in the following pages. This is a book that I wish I had found my senior year in college, for these truths were the fundamental ideas I was searching for, and they have proven invaluable in my life. After several decades of standing on these foundational truths, they have never failed to guide me in living wisely.

For those of you who are somewhat new to the Christian life, I pray that the truths will give you something to hang on to, something to anchor you when you face difficulties or hard decisions. I hope that the stories you read will flesh out for you what these truths look like in real life.

For those of you who know and love Christ, may these

truths serve as powerful reminders that although we live in a temporary world that tries to lure us into thinking that truth is determined by personal preference, God's truth and wisdom are eternal and worthy of our obedience.

When I was younger, I wanted to travel the road that would make "all the difference." I knew that I was on the right path when I meditated on this transformative truth: "Go in by the narrow gate. For the wide gate has a broad road which leads to disaster and there are many people going that way. The narrow gate and the hard road lead out into life and only a few are finding it."[3]

As a young woman, I wanted the road less traveled. I just didn't realize that it had a narrow gate and that the gate was Jesus. He is the gate that leads to life—God's life.

Proverbs 9:10 tells us, "The reverent and worshipful fear of the Lord is the beginning (the chief and choice part) of Wisdom, and the knowledge of the Holy One is insight and understanding."[4] Acknowledging that Jesus is the gate to true life and wanting to know God more intimately is foundational in learning to live wisely.

## A Prayer for Wisdom

O Lord, your way is the wise way. Thank you for being my heavenly Father who loves me for who I am, who wants to strengthen me, and who wants to teach me to live wisely for eternal purposes.

I know there is no guarantee that if I do begin to live your way, my life will become easier, but I'd rather go through the trials here on earth *with* you than without you. So, Lord, here I am—I enter by the narrow gate. In Jesus' name, amen.

# Reflections on the Truth

1. Before you read the next chapter, reflect on your own life. Where are you in your spiritual journey and your search for truth?

2. In this book, I share ten truths from Scripture that help us pursue living wisely. These truths keep me on the right path. If someone asked what your bottom-line truths are, the truths you live by, what would you say? What truths do you fall back on when you go through challenging times?

3. As you begin to read *Living Wisely,* compose a brief prayer asking God to guide you and bless you as you study his truths.

# Scripture to Believe

As the Scriptures say,

> "I will destroy human wisdom
> and discard their most brilliant ideas."

So where does this leave the philosophers, the scholars, and the world's brilliant debaters? God has made them all look foolish and has shown their wisdom to be useless nonsense.

I CORINTHIANS 1:19-20, NLT-1996

# MAYBE GOD IS RIGHT
# AFTER ALL

*Right is right, even if everyone is against it; and*
*wrong is wrong, even if everyone is for it.*
WILLIAM PENN

*For the LORD grants wisdom!*
  *From his mouth come knowledge and*
*understanding.*
PROVERBS 2:6

AS I ENTERED THE NARROW GATE and began my journey on the less-traveled road, I discovered key signposts on the path I had chosen. The more I studied, the more I realized how God's wisdom runs counter to the wisdom of the world. God asks us to trust him, to be holy, to deny ourselves, and to be generous. Our culture says: "Believe in yourself," "If it feels good, do it," "You deserve to be happy," and "The one with the most toys wins."

It's not always easy to live God's way. In fact, it's easier to go with the flow of our culture. But often, we know in our heart of hearts what is right. Sometimes we even sense the inner prompting of God's Spirit guiding us to the right path, but for any number of reasons, we tend to choose the path that is more appealing.

Such was the case with a dear woman I will call Suzanne, a married Christian who had three children. She worked as a secretary for a man who attended their family's church. Things went well for a while; then one day, Suzanne's employer took her to lunch. In subsequent months, Suzanne and her boss met more frequently, allowing themselves to be drawn into conversations that went beyond their professional association. Each of them ignored the internal voices that warned them against their growing intimacy. Suzanne and her boss followed their feelings instead of believing the truths of Scripture. Their relationship soon developed into a full-fledged affair.

After some time, Suzanne divorced her husband, hoping

to start a new life with her employer. But her boss had second thoughts about the relationship and decided not to leave his family. In the end, Suzanne was left with shattered dreams and three children to raise alone.

When I met Suzanne, three years after her divorce, it was evident that she still felt keenly the consequences of her infidelity. Now repentant and reconciled to God, she was making wise choices concerning her work and children. With tears in her eyes, she said that she still loved her husband, but the pain and betrayal were too much for him, and he was not willing to be reconciled. Suzanne lived in an "if only" world. If only she had not followed her feelings. If only she had stayed on the path God wanted her to follow. If only she had trusted that God knew what was right for her.

Suzanne is typical of so many of us who begin to believe the billboards posted on the world's broad road: "You are number one. You are the one to decide what is right for you." Our culture mocks the narrow way, chiding that it is restrictive and joyless—a dead end.

Certainly the road is narrow, but the air on this path is fresher. God's way offers a sense of freedom and peace that our world cannot duplicate. In the past, I had searched for wisdom in a secular setting, believing that other people would provide the answers to living a fulfilling, satisfying life. But the wisdom of the world failed to address my need for eternal truth that gave hope, security, and purpose. Once I encountered Christ and devoted myself to studying his Word, the wisdom of God invaded my life and opened my eyes to the thought that maybe God is right—maybe he knows what is best.

Early in my journey, I was captured by a verse in the Gospels: "I am the vine; you are the branches. Those who remain in me, and I in them, will produce much fruit. For apart from me you can do nothing."[1] I had been searching for a belief system that would guide me in making a difference in my world. Here it was. If I continued to stay closely connected to Jesus, I would be fruitful. I would grow, becoming someone who could have an impact on those around me.

The Lord's words were clear: "Apart from me you can do nothing." I thought, *Maybe God is right. Maybe he knows what he is talking about when he says that any life lived apart from him will not have any eternal significance.* It was this truth that helped me to believe that God has the authentic road map to life. Maybe the world, even with all its bravado, is wrong. The great statesman William Penn was right: "Right is right, even if everyone is against it; and wrong is wrong, even if everyone is for it."

I was beginning to wholeheartedly agree with Penn, especially by thinking that right is right even if everyone is against it. I was encouraged when I read what the Old Testament prophet Hosea says about God being right: "Let those who are wise understand these things. Let those who are discerning listen carefully. The paths of the LORD are true and right, and righteous people live by walking in them. But sinners stumble and fall along the way."[2] Yes, the Lord's paths are true and right—because *God* is right.

Jeremiah's words amplify this truth:

This is what the LORD says:
"Don't let the wise boast in their wisdom,
 or the powerful boast in their power,
 or the rich boast in their riches.
But those who wish to boast
 should boast in this alone:
that they truly know me and understand that
  I am the LORD
 who demonstrates unfailing love
 and who brings justice and righteousness to
  the earth,
and that I delight in these things.
 I, the LORD, have spoken!"[3]

I have learned over the years that true wisdom comes not from our culture and its many voices but from knowing who God is. God, above all, is righteous—good, trustworthy, blameless. If I can ever boast about anything, it is that I believe God is who he says he is. He is right. He is absolute. He is fair and just, and his love never fails. For me, discovering that God is righteous—right—in all his ways was at once humbling and reassuring. I knew that I could trust him in the midst of a frantic, mixed-up world.

When Suzanne first felt attracted to her boss, when she initially became involved in the affair, God's ways seemed restrictive and narrow to her. The command to be holy, to be faithful, to run from sexual immorality conflicted with her desires, but she didn't want to deny herself the pleasures that went with this man's attention. Any pleasure she experienced was short-lived, however. When Suzanne finally realized that her wrong choices had caused such devastating pain, she acknowledged with regret that indeed God is right after all.

One of the reasons we can trust that God is right is because we are his idea; he created us. We belong to him. The psalmist tells us, "The earth is the LORD's, and everything in it. The world and all its people belong to him."[4] It is logical to believe that since everything in the heavens and earth belongs to God, then he knows what is right for us. He has every right to tell us how to live. Who better to know the paths we should take than the one who made us?

The Bible is filled with people who learn, often too late, that God's way is the right way. Take Adam and Eve. God provided abundantly for them in the lush Garden. He gave them everything—with one restriction: He told them not to eat from the tree of the knowledge of good and evil. God's instruction was for their good. He wanted to protect them and keep them on the right path.

But in one fatal moment, Adam and Eve chose to believe a voice other than God's. First, they succumbed to Satan's deception, to his play on their self-centeredness: "Don't take God's instructions too seriously," he enticed. "Take what you want. Live life on your own terms." Adam and Eve believed him. Second, they yielded to their own rationalizations:

"Why would God deny us something that is 'good' for us? We can make our own choices."

We are still living with the consequences of Adam and Eve's refusal to follow God's instructions. After they ate the forbidden fruit, they realized they had sinned.[5] As they hid from God, I can imagine that they said to one another, "Maybe God was right after all."

Adam and Eve weren't the only people who suffered the consequences of thinking God can't possibly know what's best. When God directed Moses to take the Israelites into Canaan, a land the Lord had prepared for his children, they rebelled and did not enter the land. They relied on their own insight and refused the path God had for them. I cannot help but think that as the Israelites trudged through the wilderness for forty years, many of them whispered to one another, "Maybe God was right after all."

Jesus reiterated this truth in a story he told about a young Jewish man who demanded his inheritance from his father and left to live life on his own terms.[6] Again in this story, the father provided everything the son needed, but the son thought he knew better. He took his inheritance and spent it on wild living. We can only imagine the parties, the women, the food the young man indulged in, hoping to find satisfaction. When his inheritance was spent, however, the young man was reduced to a pitiful life of feeding pigs. It was then that he concluded, *Maybe my father was right after all*. He turned from his sinful ways, returned home, and asked for his father's forgiveness.

Jesus used the story to teach his listeners that God, our Father, knows what is best for his children. When we trust that he is right and follow his ways, we experience God's protection and provision and can avoid unnecessary consequences.

When I consider the revolutionary life Jesus led, I realize that even though he was God in the flesh, he modeled for us the truth that his Father is right. Jesus shared this thought with his disciples: "I have come down from heaven to do the will of God who sent me, not to do what I want."[7] That truth was as extraordinary in Jesus' day as it is today.

Jesus perfectly exemplifies for us the truth that wanting to live God's way brings joy. God said to his beloved Son, "You love what is right and hate what is wrong. Therefore God, your God, has anointed you, pouring out the oil of joy on you more than on anyone else."[8]

After speaking at a conference, I was able to share this truth with "Lillian," who was driving me to the airport. She shared her concern about a broken relationship. A woman at her church had hurt her with an unkind, offhand remark at a group meeting. Lillian struggled with what to do. She wanted to hide whenever she saw this woman, and she knew that wasn't right. As I listened, I asked Lillian if she had gone to the person in order to seek reconciliation.

Lillian answered, "No. I sought counsel from our group leader, and she offered to handle it for me. So far nothing has been resolved."

I then said, "You know, maybe God is right when he

taught that if someone sins against *you*, then you are the one to go to that person." I read her the passage in Matthew: "If another believer sins against you, go privately and point out the fault. If the other person listens and confesses it, you have won that person back."[9] We discussed how she might pray and ask God to show her the path to reconciliation.

A week later, I received a letter from Lillian. "I was encouraged to go to the person who hurt me because of the Scripture you shared with me. I am praying that God will use it for good. It was not easy for me, but the person was humbled and receptive. I am praising God."

As I read her letter, I thought once more, *Maybe God is right after all.*

Carolyn lived next door to a cantankerous neighbor who had a pit bull. If the dog had been fenced in, it would not have been such a problem, but there was nothing separating her yard from her neighbor's. The pit bull was a continual annoyance to both Carolyn and her dog.

One day, when she was discussing the problem with her neighbor—who had a personality similar to his dog's—he became belligerent and said some harsh things. Feeling hurt and angry, Carolyn went back into her house. As she stewed, a verse from Scripture came to her mind: "Bless those who curse you. Pray for those who hurt you."[10] Praying for that man was the last thing Carolyn wanted to do, but she was receptive to God's instructions. Pray she did, and her anger subsided.

A few days later when she was out walking her dog, the

neighbor came out and apologized: "You know, I shouldn't have spoken to you the way I did. I was wrong."

As Carolyn told me this story, I found myself remarking, "Isn't it great to know that God is right after all?"

In my own life, I continually have to acknowledge that God's truths are right. I once visited a good friend who had just remodeled her home. It was beautiful and had everything I think a home should have, including a paneled library and a huge walk-in closet with built-in shelves and drawers. When I left her home, I was somewhat depressed. Actually, I was envious. I thought, *Lord, I would really enjoy living in a home like that. I wish I had one that nice.* Then a verse I had memorized marched to the forefront of my mind and demanded my attention: Love "does not envy."[11] I was lovingly and justly rebuked. God was teaching me that if I truly love, I will not envy.

God amazingly restores and redeems us even when we choose to believe that maybe we are right. I am astounded by God's grace to his children when we do not live his way. He takes our sinful self-absorption and patiently waits to redirect our lives. Adam and Eve had to leave the Garden, but God continued to lead them and bless them. The Israelites had to wander in the wilderness, but God continued to guide them and provide for their needs. The young Jewish man returned home and continued to live as his father's beloved son. God's grace restored Suzanne to the true and right path, and his care for me tenderly teaches me not to envy. Because God created us and redeemed us by Christ's death on the cross, he wants us to understand that he is committed to leading us to live wisely.

*Look, God is all-powerful.*
*Who is a teacher like him?*
*No one can tell him what to do,*
*or say to him, "You have done wrong."*

JOB 36:22-23

# A Prayer for Wisdom

Heavenly Father, while I am here on this earth, I want to stay on the paths you have marked out for me because I know that I would not be content anywhere else. I want to boast that I know and understand that you alone are just and righteous. Keep me from presuming that I know the best way. Please show me your ways, and prompt me to choose your true and right paths. I don't want to go through life tripping and stumbling.

Thank you for your unfailing love and grace when I question the path I'm on. Keep me on this less-traveled road—for my life is yours, and I want what is right in your Kingdom, even if everyone else is against it. In Jesus' name, amen.

# Reflections on the Truth

1. As you think back over your life, you probably can remember times when you thought your way was better than God's way. Explain one of these times and the consequences of your actions.

2. You probably can also remember a time when following God's way ultimately worked for your good. Describe this experience.

3. God's ways are not your ways—and therefore your trust must be grounded in confidence that his ways are best. What do the following passages teach you about God's ways?

   a. Deuteronomy 32:4

   b. Psalm 18:30

   c. Psalm 33:4-5

4. God wants to be intimately involved in your life. What do these verses say to encourage you to walk the Lord's paths?

   a. Psalm 25:8-10

   b. Psalm 23:1-3

   c. Proverbs 28:26

5. "The LORD is good and does what is right."[12] What situation in your life needs direction at the moment? Write out a prayer asking God to lead you on the right path.

## Scripture to Believe

But for those who are righteous,
    the way is not steep and rough.
You are a God who does what is right,
    and you smooth out the path ahead of them.

ISAIAH 26:7

# GOD IS FOR YOU,
# NOT AGAINST YOU

*At once, the Cross revealed what kind of world we have and what kind of God we have: a world of gross unfairness, a God of sacrificial love.*

PHILIP YANCEY, *Disappointment with God*


*Can anything ever separate us from Christ's love? Does it mean he no longer loves us if we have trouble or calamity, or are persecuted, or hungry, or destitute, or in danger, or threatened with death? . . . No, despite all these things, overwhelming victory is ours through Christ, who loved us.*

ROMANS 8:35-37

BELIEVING THAT GOD IS right after all keeps us on the narrow path and from traveling on the broad road that ultimately leads to regret for living selfishly. But walking this well-trodden, narrow way carries no guarantee that our lives will be free from suffering. At one point, Jesus summed up what he had been teaching by saying, "I have told you all this so that you may have peace in me. Here on earth you will have many trials and sorrows. But take heart, because I have overcome the world."[1] No matter which road we choose to travel, trials and sorrows are part of the journey. Jesus taught, "He gives his sunlight to both the evil and the good, and he sends rain on the just and the unjust alike."[2]

My dear friend Nancy's young husband, Ron, died of pancreatic cancer, leaving her alone with two boys, one with special needs. Jack and I met Ron when he was single and in the air force. It was a joy to watch the Lord bring Nancy into his life and then to see their trust and love grow when their handicapped son was born. They settled in New Mexico, bought a lovely home, and were walking on the true and right path.

After Ron died, Nancy focused on taking care of her boys and moving through her grief. Less than five months later, she learned the devastating news that her mother had been diagnosed with pancreatic cancer also. An only child, she traveled to be with her mother, her grief over Ron's death still fresh. While she was with her parents, Nancy discovered that her father had Alzheimer's and would need special care.

It was at this point that she fell on her knees and asked the question, *God, are you for me or against me?*

When we encounter seemingly insurmountable road-blocks and the way becomes hard and lonely, we cannot help but wonder why God's path would lead to such heartache and pain and we cannot help but ask, "Why do bad things happen to good people?"

Sometimes our own hearts echo the same question: *God, how can I believe your love is unfailing when trials and heart-aches crush my spirit and threaten to leave me hopeless? How can I say you are for me, Lord, when everything seems to be against me?*

In the context of these understandable yet piercing questions, choosing to believe that God is for you and not against you can be difficult.

Two sisters in the New Testament struggled to believe that the Lord was for them. Mary, Martha, and their brother, Lazarus, knew Jesus intimately because he was often a guest in their home. At one point in Jesus' relationship with them, Lazarus became critically ill, and Martha and Mary sent word to the Lord that Lazarus was sick. But surprisingly, Jesus did not rush to their house. The Gospel account of the story tells us: "Although Jesus loved Martha, Mary, and Lazarus, he stayed where he was for the next two days."[3]

When Jesus did finally arrive in Bethany, Martha met him and told him: "Lord, if only you had been here, my brother would not have died. But even now I know that God will give you whatever you ask."[4] Martha believed in Jesus and

expressed her hope in him, but the implication in her statement was, "You are late. I know you love us, but are you for
us or against us? I think that if you were for us, you would
have been here sooner."

This is what is so hard with believing that God is for us:
Grief and pain can overpower us and cause us to doubt God's
love and care. If God doesn't come through for us the way
we want him to, then we conclude he must be against us. It
is easy to believe that if we are committed to walking God's
paths, then he owes us a good, trouble-free life.

Several years ago, my friend Page was at a crisis point in
her life. After twelve years in the mission field, she was in the
process of packing up her family for their permanent move
back to the States to be near her mom and dad. Page and
her husband had chosen to live near her parents because she
wanted to build a relationship with her mother—something
she had never had. It was an emotional upheaval to say good-
bye to dear friends, finish ministry projects, and endure a
twenty-seven-hour flight home. On the night of their depar-
ture, she received a phone call telling her that her mother
had fallen, suffered a cerebral hemorrhage, and was on life
support. Page's first thought was, *This can't be happening.
Mom and Dad are supposed to pick us up at the airport tomorrow. This must be some cruel joke. I've been gone twelve years,
and finally when I'm coming back—on the eve of our return,
no less—Mom is about to die?*

Page's mother did die. After the funeral and settling into a
new area, my friend realized that she needed to deal with her

disappointment with God. She was angry, not only that her mother had died but also for the loss of the renewed relationship she had hoped to have with her mom. She thought, *God owes me. Big time.* She scheduled a three-day silent retreat and told God, "I want either an explanation or an apology." For two days, she sat in angry silence. On the third day, she went for a walk and observed a deep, calm pool of water. As she stared at the water, she heard God whisper, *I want you to go deeper with me.*

When she returned to the cabin, she was finally ready to receive what the Lord wanted to tell her. One of God's thoughts to her was this: *My daughter, I have watched you chase after your mother's blessing for years. You have been unrelenting in your pursuit, even while overseas. And you have been angry. I have been here the whole time. I want to bless you. I always have. But you have valued your mother's blessing over mine. You have refused to see that. The blessing your soul has been seeking is mine to give. You are my daughter whom I love; with you I am well pleased.*[5]

The challenge for my friend was to accept God's love and to believe how much he was *for* her. She began to see that our circumstances are not an accurate indicator of God's goodness. In fact, God had been longing to let her know how much he was for her, how much he loved her, how much he wanted to bless her in the midst of her pain and loneliness.

God is for us. Isn't this the all-encompassing, extraordinary message of the Cross? God was so determined to show us that he is for us that he sent his own Son to earth to reveal his character and redeem a lost world. The apostle John wrote, "God showed how much he loved us by sending his one and only Son into the world so that we might have eternal life through him. This is real love—not that we loved God, but that he loved us and sent his Son as a sacrifice to take away our sins."[6]

This is the good news: God loves us unconditionally, and the Cross is his proclamation throughout the ages that he is for us. Oswald Chambers wrote, "The centre of salvation is the Cross of Jesus, and the reason it is so easy to obtain salvation is because it cost God so much. The Cross is the point where God and sinful man merge with a crash and the way to life is opened—but the crash is on the heart of God."[7]

The Cross became necessary because our first parents, Adam and Eve, were not convinced that God was for them. They turned away from God and went their own way.

We, too, are prone to abandon God, but that doesn't alter the truth that God is for us. Isaiah assured us of this when he wrote,

He was pierced for our rebellion,
    crushed for our sins.
He was beaten so we could be whole.
    He was whipped so we could be healed.
All of us, like sheep, have strayed away.
    We have left God's paths to follow our own.
Yet the LORD laid on him
    the sins of us all.[8]

When we believe and accept by faith the redemption accomplished through Christ's sacrifice, he rescues us and saves us. When we admit our need for a Savior and ask Jesus to come into our lives, he reconciles us to himself and adopts us into his family. We are then free to walk his path through this troubled world, trusting his grace and love to be enough for us.

When you face overwhelming circumstances and wonder if God is for you, hear him say to you the words of commitment he said to his people thousands of years ago:

Do not be afraid, for I have ransomed you.
　　I have called you by name; you are mine.
When you go through deep waters,
　　I will be with you.
When you go through rivers of difficulty,
　　you will not drown.
When you walk through the fire of oppression,
　　you will not be burned up;
　　the flames will not consume you.
For I am the LORD, your God,
　　the Holy One of Israel, your Savior.[9]

Lieutenant Colonel Brian Birdwell was in the Pentagon on September 11, 2001, when American Airlines Flight 77 crashed into the building. He was standing fifteen to twenty yards from the point of impact and was burned on more than 60 percent of his body. His wife, Mel, was his constant companion as he journeyed an extremely painful road back to health. She writes,

There were many times when I would tell God, "I do not like this path, and you need to change it." And God's love for us is so amazing that he would reply, *I understand your anger. I feel it too about what happened to Brian. But I won't change this path. However, I will walk down it with you.*

That wasn't the answer I wanted to hear! But I did find comfort knowing that no matter what I did and said or how belligerent I became with God, he always loved me.[10]

God tenderly spoke to Mel about his love and faithfulness to be with them during their river of difficulty. He also speaks to you. Through the Cross, God ransomed you and promised to be with you through every difficulty. You will go through deep waters, but you are not alone, and you will not be overwhelmed. His concern is for your spiritual welfare as you walk through the fire. Our inner strength cannot be burned up or consumed because he is for us.

When I visited with my friend Nancy and asked how she was doing, she said, "The pain was almost unbearable, but deep down in my heart I knew that God understood how I felt. I held on to the fact that God loved me. It didn't look as if he did, and it didn't feel as if he did, but the Cross and his Spirit were an ever-present reminder of his love and care. I thought that if I let go of God, what would I have left? Who else could I turn to?"

Maybe you have experienced some similarly overwhelming

trials. Or maybe you are more like me. My difficulties have not been as catatrosphic as many have had to endure. But I am well acquainted with adversity and have learned that whether the trials I go through are major upheavals or minor intrusions, God is always there for me.

Years ago, God used a relatively inconsequential incident in my life to reinforce this truth. My father was slowly dying of congestive heart failure in Houston, and I made frequent trips from my home in Tucson to visit him and to support my mother. After one particular visit, I helped my mom get my dad into the car so that she could take him to a doctor's appointment after driving me to the airport. When we arrived, I hugged and kissed them both, quickly got out of the car, and tearfully watched them drive away, for I was never sure if I would see my dad again.

As I walked up to the ticket counter to check in for my flight, my heart stopped: I had left my plane tickets on the backseat of the car (this was before computerized ticketing and cell phones). I was devastated. In my heart, I immediately expressed my feelings to God: *Lord, with all I have on my plate right now, couldn't you oversee some of these minor details?*

After buying a one-way ticket (which was eventually reimbursed), I went to the gate and waited for my flight to depart. It was then that I heard the Lord speak his thoughts to my heart: *Cynthia, do you think that I love you less because life is not being lived on your terms right now? You need to understand that life cannot always be as you would like. You cannot judge my love for you by how well your life is going. My desire is that when you encounter trials, you would turn to me in dependence and trust. Let me be all you need when you feel disappointed and alone. Be steadfast and know that I will never leave you or forsake you. I, above everyone else, will always be for you.*

And so I have begun to understand this wonderful truth of God's love and grace. Focusing only on my circumstances can certainly lead down the path of discouragement, but believing that I have God's presence and peace as I go through trials can make all the difference in my journey. What I encounter here in my travels is really only temporary. The Cross reminds me that I am bound for eternity. In what greater way could God demonstrate his love? How can God ever be against us when he died for us?

> *The greatest sorrow and burden you can lay on the Father, the greatest unkindness you can do to him, is not to believe that he loves you.*
> JOHN OWEN, *Communion with God*

# A Prayer for Wisdom

Heavenly Father, when I look at the Cross, I am awestruck by the lavish outpouring of your grace and love. I am humbled by your sacrifice. I know that I am a sinner saved by your grace alone, and I am grateful and penitent all at once.

Yet, Lord, why do I so easily forget your love and what you have done for me? Why do I let the hurts and difficulties I face cloud your desire to comfort me, strengthen me, and give me peace? O Lord, help this independent child to live continually in the truth that you are the only one who loves me unconditionally and who will never leave me or forsake me. In every way possible, you are *for* me. In Jesus' name, amen.

# Reflections on the Truth

1. C. S. Lewis said, "God loves us; not because we are loveable but because He is love, not because he needs to receive but because He delights to give."[11] In what ways do the following verses communicate God's love? How do the verses comfort you in your discouragement and strengthen your ability to trust that God is for you?

   a. Psalm 56:9

   b. Psalm 103:8-14

   c. Psalm 118:5-9

   d. Psalm 139:17-18

2. Tribulations are part of the world's landscape. As you read these verses, write down how God promises to help you as you go through trials.

    a. Psalm 18:31-36

    b. Isaiah 41:10

    c. Romans 8:31-39

3. The Cross is God's way of proclaiming his love for the world. How can embracing the reality of God's sacrificial love and care change the way you persevere through trials?

4. God's message given through the prophet Isaiah is as real for you today as it was for Israel. As you read the passage, personalize it. Fill in the blanks with your name and the details of your circumstances. Then hear God's loving words of comfort to you:

But now, O [your name], listen to the LORD who created you.
    O [your name], the one who formed you says,
"Do not be afraid, for I have ransomed you.
    I have called you by name; you are mine.
When you go through [your circumstances],
    I will be with you.
When you go through rivers of [your difficulty],
    you will not drown.
When you walk through the fire of [your problem],
    you will not be burned up;
    the flames will not consume you.
For I am the LORD, your God,
    the Holy One of Israel, your Savior. . . .
You are precious to me.
    You are honored, and I love you.
"Do not be afraid, for I am with you."[12]

5. As you review this chapter and the Scripture verses, what encouragement have you received to live wisely?

## Scripture to Believe

What shall we say about such wonderful things as these? If God is for us, who can ever be against us? Since he did not spare even his own Son but gave him up for us all, won't he also give us everything else?

ROMANS 8:31-32

# THREE

# TRUST GOD, EVEN WHEN IT DOESN'T MAKE SENSE

*Our task is not to decipher exactly how all of life's pieces fit*
*and what they all mean but to remain faithful and obedient*
*to God, who knows all mysteries. That is the kind of faith*
*that is pleasing to God—a faith that is determined to trust*
*him when he has not answered all the questions, when we*
*have not heard the voice from the whirlwind.*

NANCY GUTHRIE, *Holding On to Hope*

*Blessed are those who trust in the LORD*
    *and have made the LORD their hope and confidence.*
    *They are like trees planted along a riverbank,*
    *with roots that reach deep into the water.*
    *Such trees are not bothered by the heat*
    *or worried by long months of drought.*
    *Their leaves stay green,*
    *and they never stop producing fruit.*

JEREMIAH 17:7-8

ON THE DAY AFTER the birth of Nancy and David Guthrie's second child, Hope, a geneticist came to tell them that their newborn had Zellweger syndrome—a rare congenital neurological disorder that would lead to their daughter's death, probably within months. They were stunned. They cared for Hope through seizures and close calls. They loved her passionately. And after only 199 days, they buried her.[1]

Nancy and David's faith was strong, but their faith didn't make their loss hurt any less. Because of their desire to protect their older son and their parents from such a sorrowful, distressing experience again, they took surgical steps to prevent future pregnancies. Inexplicably, though, Nancy became pregnant again, and they discovered through prenatal tests that the baby boy growing inside her also had the deadly syndrome. As the Guthries anticipated the delivery of their baby, they knew what to expect this time: the joy of loving their son and the incredible agony of losing him. Nancy writes, "Even though we don't understand, and it is so dark we cannot see to take a step forward, we can choose to hang on, to keep trusting, to keep believing God's Word."[2]

Because the Guthries knew that God was for them, not against them, they chose to trust God even when it didn't make sense. Choosing to "hang on" to God in the midst of intense heartache takes a determined faith. The apostle Peter wrote: "My purpose in writing is to encourage you and assure you that the grace of God is with you no matter what happens."[3] Biblical trust believes in God's presence, strength, and grace to sustain us—no matter what happens. Trust chooses to have resolute faith and confidence in God's ability to work every circumstance that comes into our lives for our good and his glory. This trust is filled with hope, peace, and a sense of abandonment—an abandonment that frees us from carrying our burdens alone and joins us with Christ, who will walk with us through our trial.

Elisabeth Elliot understood what it meant to trust God when it doesn't make sense. When she was first married, she and her husband Jim Elliot served as missionaries in Ecuador. In 1956, Jim and four other missionaries were seeking to make contact with the Auca Indians. During one of their initial encounters, Jim and the others were senselessly killed. It was a devastating loss for Elisabeth. After staying in Ecuador for a period of time, serving the Indians, she returned to the United States and later married Addison Leitch, a seminary professor. When she and Addison learned that he had cancer, she said to God, "You can't be serious." She couldn't believe God would "allow her to be a widow again." She remembers his voice responding, *And if I am?* She knew those words were God's challenge for her to trust him. And she did—even when it didn't make sense.[4]

Addison eventually went to be with the Lord, but Elisabeth once again found that Christ's presence on her journey was enough. She later wrote,

The trail is steep and very rocky, and gets steeper and rockier the nearer it gets to the summit. The company of a friend does not make the distance shorter, but it makes it seem shorter. It doesn't eliminate any of the rocks, but the rocks don't seem so terribly daunting. The glad receiving of the yoke of Christ halves our life's burden. The road is still a tough one, but the roughness won't matter nearly so much.[5]

Many people in our world today believe that trusting God even when it doesn't make sense is foolish at best. Choosing to stay on the steep and narrow road, choosing to keep on hoping when all seems hopeless, choosing to trust when all the questions are not answered—this is the road less traveled.

The old patriarch Job—who suffered the loss of his wealth, his children, and his health—held on to his faith even when his wife told him to give up on God. As Job sat on the ash heap, scraping the boils on his skin, his wife said, "Are you still trying to maintain your integrity? Curse God and die."[6] Conventional wisdom, even from family and friends, says to blame God, to give up. It warns us not to become religious fanatics. It urges us to go it alone because who knows what happens when we trust God.

Job's reply to his wife is intriguing: "You talk like a godless woman. Should we accept only good things from the hand of God and never anything bad?"[7] Here is our dilemma: It is relatively easy to trust God when all of life's pieces fit together, but it becomes an enormous challenge to trust him when life falls apart.

Tucked away in the Old Testament is a memorable

account of a young woman whose life suddenly fell apart. Jochebed and her husband, Amram, had two children: Aaron and Miriam. Her life was not easy; she and the other Hebrews were slaves in Egypt. But her life became quite complicated when she gave birth to a second son. The problem was that the pharaoh had issued an edict that all male Hebrew babies were to be killed at birth. What were her options in this incredibly difficult trial? Perhaps she voiced her turmoil in this way: "I feel that this child is special, but I don't understand why he was born now—it doesn't make sense."

But Jochebed chose to trust God, and she kept her baby hidden—at great risk. Then, when he was three months old, she placed him in a basket and set him among the reeds at the river's edge. When the Egyptian princess came to the river, she found the baby and was touched by his cries. In a miraculous series of events, the princess decided to save the baby's life and ended up hiring the baby's mother to nurse the infant. The princess named the baby boy Moses, meaning "to lift out," because she had taken him out of the river. If you are familiar with the Old Testament, you know the significant role Moses played in leading God's people out of slavery into the Promised Land.[8]

Maybe you are currently facing some circumstances that don't make sense. What will you do? What are your choices?

The Guthries could have become bitter at God and turned away from their faith. Job could have cursed God and died. Jochebed could have become distraught, depressed, and overwhelmed by her circumstances. They could have, but they didn't. Instead, the Guthries held on to their faith. Job restlessly pursued God and heard his voice in the whirlwind. Jochebed trusted God by leaving Moses in a handmade ark, floating at the water's edge of the Nile River.

But it is not easy to maintain a steadfast faith when circumstances become overpowering and inescapable. Such was the experience of Jane, a woman I met at a conference. With tears in her eyes, she approached me and began to tell me her story. She had been a Christian since childhood, but her life had begun to fall apart. Her young husband was diagnosed with cancer, could no longer work, and was experiencing depression. In order to support their family of three children, Jane was working many twelve-hour shifts as a nurse. The weight she was carrying began to crush her spirit, and she felt as if she could no longer hold on to her faith. She found it hard to trust God. She felt hopeless and alone.

I embraced this precious young woman and wept with her. I so wanted to make her life right. I so wanted God to lift her burden. I so wanted to give her an answer that would instantly give her hope. Her feelings were certainly understandable, so much so that I wanted to protectively stand in front of her and tell God that he was giving her more than she could bear. After I prayed with her, though, I took her hand and asked her a question that I have asked myself many times when I have been overcome by circumstances and felt that my back was against the wall.

My question was this: "Jane, what are your options? You can continue your journey alone, relying on your own strength, trying to make your life work apart from God. You can blame God for your heartache and suffering, and turn your back on him. But is this the best way to walk this difficult road? At this point in your life, what have you to lose by choosing to trust God—even when it doesn't make sense?"

As Jane considered these questions, she eventually whispered, "Nothing. I have nothing to lose by trusting God. Perhaps I have everything to gain."

Nancy Guthrie voices these same thoughts:

The truth is, there is no comfort to be found
away from God; at least, there is no lasting, deep,
satisfying comfort. Revenge, ritual, retreat—they
don't bring any lasting relief from the pain. Only the
truth of God's Word, the tenderness of his welcome,
the touch of his healing presence bring the kind of
comfort we crave. Only his promises of purpose in
this life and perfection in the life to come offer us
any kind of real hope to hold on to.

Do you find yourself wanting to leave the faith
you've claimed now that it has been put to the
test of adversity? So where will you go? In your
discouragement, where will you find the comfort
you so desperately crave?[9]

In the midst of a crushing test of adversity, my friend Carol Kent has found that her faith and trust have carried her through her deep trial. Carol's only child, a graduate of the

United States Naval Academy and a young man who loves God, was sentenced to life in prison without parole on a murder charge. In her book *When I Lay My Isaac Down*, she shares,

> All of us have circumstances that produce varying degrees of personal loss and devastation. Will we maintain our grip on hope in the process of defeat? Will we live our lives with passion and purpose even if, in this lifetime, we are not permitted to have an answer to why something has happened? Will we choose unshakable faith, or will we give up on God? I believe God's great invitation is to engage us in the process of discovering the power of choosing faith when that decision makes no sense. There is hidden power in our unthinkable circumstances.[10]

Lisa Beamer also chose to trust God even when it didn't make sense. On September 11, 2001, Lisa's husband, Todd, died while helping to divert one of the planes hijacked by terrorists. She was left to raise her two sons and soon-to-be-born daughter without Todd, her very best friend. Lisa writes,

> The pain is real, but so is the hope. . . .
> Hope comes from knowing who *is* in control. Hope comes from knowing that we have a sovereign, loving God who is in control of every event of our lives. . . . In the book of Jeremiah (29:11) it says that

God has a plan for me, a plan to prosper me and not to harm me; a plan to give me a hope and a future. And that is what holds me together every day when I get out of bed in the morning: to know that is true, and it has been proven true in my life to date. It was true on September 11, and it will be true for as many years as God has left for me. . . .

. . . I have found safety and security in a loving heavenly Father, who cannot be shaken, who will never leave me or forsake me, and in whom I can trust completely.[11]

The essence of trust is confidence in the Lord's promise to ultimately prosper us and not harm us, to give us a hope and a future. This kind of trust can be hard work, though, for it involves the unknown and the unexplainable. This kind of trust means choosing to remain faithful to the God who "knows all mysteries." Many times, I have cried out to the Lord, asking him to explain or change my circumstances for the better, and his standard response is always, *Cynthia, do you trust me?* My standard reply is, "Yes, Lord, I will trust you if you'll just tell me how this is going to turn out." The Lord quickly responds, *Cynthia, if I tell you how it will turn out, then there will be no need for you to trust.*

We don't like mystery. We're much more comfortable with certainty than with uncertainty. Paula Rinehart, a marriage and family counselor, writes,

Indeed, any serious grappling with trust will lead us to the heart of mystery, of all that God chooses not to tell us. And mystery, as someone once said, is an embarrassment to the modern mind. . . .

. . . But accepting the mystery of what we cannot know will lead us to the heart of God where we trade our craving for explanation for a simple willingness to trust.[12]

When our circumstances force us to come to God, what we find is mystery—the majestic mystery of God's sovereignty, love, and trustworthiness. It is in the dark that trust becomes trust. It is when the questions are not answered that trust blesses us and pleases God. The verse quoted at the beginning of this chapter is such an encouragement: "Blessed are those who trust in the LORD and have made the LORD their hope and confidence." Those who trust the Lord become like trees that are strong and can weather any storm. They are beautiful, always green and producing delicious fruit. Our trust is not in vain, for God's plan is to prosper us and to bring beauty out of ashes. He is the only one who can.

Trust is precious and indispensable during our times of suffering, but trust also involves stepping out by faith into the unknown. I usually smile when I read the Old Testament account of the Israelites crossing the Jordan River in order to occupy the Promised Land. Joshua asked the priests to carry the Ark ahead of the people, and the priests' assignment was to start walking into the swollen river. It was necessary for the priests to get their feet wet before the waters would part. I can just imagine the look on the priests' faces! Trust often involves "getting our feet wet."

Many years ago, Jack and I crossed our own Jordan in order to enter a new land. As I mentioned before, in the early 1970s, Jack felt God calling him to sell his practice and join the staff of a Christian organization. Serving with this group meant raising our own support and depending on monthly donations for income. We didn't make our decision lightly. We had four children, two dogs, two cats, and a parakeet to provide for, so we were somewhat anxious and excited at the same time.

When we told our friends and family what we were planning to do, they were not all that enthusiastic. It just didn't make sense to them. They had lots of questions: "How can you walk away from a thriving practice?" "How can you leave your friends?" "How are you going to provide for a family of six?"

God does bless those who trust in him. He has faithfully met our needs over all these years, and so far, our leaves are still green. Jack and I have often been encouraged by the words of George Mueller, an evangelist who founded orphanages and depended fully on God for all their needs:

Be assured, if you walk with Him, look to Him, and expect help from Him, He will never fail you. An older believer who has known the Lord for forty-four years wrote the following as an encouragement to you: "God has never failed me. Even in my greatest difficulties, heaviest trials, and deepest poverty and need, He has never failed me. Because I was enabled by God's grace to trust Him, He has always come to my aid. I delight in speaking well of His name."[13]

And so, dear friend, I also delight in speaking well of his name, for I have trusted him now for over fifty years. This has not been a stoic trust but a trust based on God's character to faithfully bless, comfort, and produce his fruit in my life. "Accepting the mystery of what we cannot know" has enabled me to hold on to his hand when the way was dark and I needed to get my feet wet.

One of my favorite passages in Scripture is this statement of faith: "Whom have I in heaven but you? I desire you more than anything on earth. My health may fail, and my spirit may grow weak, but God remains the strength of my heart; he is mine forever."[14] It is God who strengthens me and enables me to trust so that I can endure months of drought and the heat of the day.

Blessed are those who trust in the Lord. Blessed, joyful, pleased, contented is everyone who trusts God—especially when it doesn't make sense. It is the best and wisest way to live.

*There is nothing, indeed, which God will not
do for a man who dares to step out upon what
seems to be the mist; though as he puts down
his foot he finds a rock beneath him.*

F. B. MEYER, quoted in *Streams in the Desert*

# A Prayer for Wisdom

Heavenly Father, trust is for my benefit, isn't it? When
you ask me to trust, you are freeing me to experience
you in deeper ways and to see you work in my life. You
are freeing me from having to rely on myself. When I
trust, I know that I'm not alone and that I don't have
to understand everything that happens. I can rest in
your love and plan for me. Thank you for leading me
in your true and right path, where I have received
many blessings I think I would have missed if I had
trusted in myself.

Thank you for being my rock, my fortress, my deliverer
all these years. Your grace has been more than sufficient.
I pray that I can spend the rest of my life continuing to
grow as a tree along your riverbank, letting my roots grow
deep into the water because my hope and confidence are
in you. Truly you are mine forever. Amen.

# Reflections on the Truth

1. Life is often a mystery and doesn't make sense. What have been some of your circumstances that haven't made sense? How did you respond, and what was the result?

2. The Scriptures encourage our trust and give us examples of those who trusted when it didn't make sense. How do the following passages strengthen you to trust God in your difficult circumstances?

   a. Psalm 143:7-10

   b. Isaiah 26:3-4

   c. Daniel 6:19-23

3. As you review this chapter, what truths will help you make the Lord your hope and confidence? Prayerfully express these truths, asking God to apply them to your life.

# Scripture to Believe

Blessed are those who trust in the LORD
and have made the LORD their hope and confidence.

They are like trees planted along a riverbank,
    with roots that reach deep into the water.
Such trees are not bothered by the heat
    or worried by long months of drought.
Their leaves stay green,
    and they never stop producing fruit.

JEREMIAH 17:7-8

# FREEDOM FROM SELF
# IS A CHOICE

*The true value of a human being is determined primarily by the measure and the sense in which he has attained liberation from the self.*

ALBERT EINSTEIN

*Then he said to the crowd, "If any of you wants to be my follower, you must turn from your selfish ways, take up your cross daily, and follow me. If you try to hang on to your life, you will lose it. But if you give up your life for my sake, you will save it."*

LUKE 9:23-24, NLT-2007

WHEN I READ THE "ABOUT THE AUTHOR" page in Robertson McQuilkin's book *A Promise Kept*, I was struck by the fact that the first accomplishment mentioned is that he was a homemaker. McQuilkin was also the former president of Columbia Bible College and Seminary, a former missionary to Japan, and a writer and conference speaker. How did this teacher of ethics and hermeneutics become a homemaker? It is an intriguing and inspirational story.

Robertson's wife, Muriel, the mother of six children, was the host of a radio program, a gifted artist, a counselor, and a wonderful helper to her husband. At the age of fifty-five, though, she began to exhibit signs of early Alzheimer's. Over the years, as the disease progressed and Muriel became more dependent on her husband, Robertson realized that he needed to resign his position at the college and be available to care for his wife.

In his letter of resignation, he explained:

My dear wife, Muriel, has been in failing mental health for about 12 years. . . . Recently it has become apparent that Muriel is contented most of the time when she is with me and almost none of the time I am away from her. It is not just "discontent." She is filled with fear—even terror—that she has lost me and always goes in search of me when I leave home. So it is clear to me that she needs me now, full-time. . . .

. . . She has cared for me fully and sacrificially all these years; if I cared for her for the next 40 years I would not be out of her debt. Duty, however, can be grim and stoic. But there is more; I love Muriel. She is a delight to me. . . . I don't *have* to care for her. I *get* to! It is a high honor to care for so wonderful a person.[1]

The Phillips translation of Luke 9:23 resounds in Dr. McQuilkin's life: "If anyone wants to follow in my footsteps, he must give up all right to himself. . . ."[2] This Christian leader gave up the right to himself, embraced the will of God, and followed the true and right path that God had for him. He said that the choice was easy because the path was so clear.

McQuilkin was quick to acknowledge that his decision to leave his position to become a homemaker is not the only or the best approach for everyone. Many people are unable to care for loved ones because of financial, physical, or emotional constraints, but this was the right choice for his life. Because it was such an extraordinary choice, it elicited responses that typify the thinking of a society centered on self: "You can't leave your ministry! God needs you where you are." "Others can take care of your wife. You have to think of yourself." "You need a life of your own." "She really doesn't even know you at this point; she will never miss you." "You are too valuable to just stay home!"

This bent to promote, protect, and exalt self starts early in life. One of the first phrases our children said was, "Me first!"

Because our self-centeredness is so inbred, Jesus made it clear that if we want to follow him, we must give up our "selves." Eugene Peterson's paraphrase of this verse in Luke states that we are not in the driver's seat.[3] An analogy that helped me understand the meaning and process of laying aside myself uses this same imagery of a car: When we are born, we are given a car to drive down the highway of life. When I was twelve years old, I stopped my car and invited Christ into my life. I was sincere in accepting Christ as my personal Savior, but because of my limited understanding, I put him in the back seat, and I stayed in the driver's seat. When I was twenty-six, my life consisted of three small children born in three years, an extremely busy husband off delivering calves and poodles, a very old house with rats, and little fellowship. It was at this time that I told the Lord that I was struggling, exhausted, and overwhelmed. As I was still before him, what I heard was this: *Cynthia, will you give the steering wheel of your life to me? Will you move over and let me drive?* I knew what the Lord was asking of me: "Lay aside your old self that cares only about what is good for you. Surrender your life into my care, and let me 'drive' you on the true and right path. Only on my path will you find your true self."

For me, it was an easy choice. What did I have to lose by letting the Lord control my life? I was weary of trying to live life in my own strength and was ready to accept God's offer. It can be frightening to let someone else drive, but I knew that God loved me, was for me, and could be trusted. So I took my hands off the steering wheel, moved over, and expected some monumental upheaval in my life. What happened, though, was that none of my circumstances changed; what changed was *me*. Everything was different. It wasn't an instant change but a progressive one, even until this day. I slowly became free from the old self that continually drove me around, demanding that my needs and welfare were most important and that life should be lived on my terms. I eventually realized that I no longer felt "put upon" by my husband, children, or even God.

What I was experiencing was freedom—freedom from my old sinful self. The freedom that Christ's sacrifice on the cross purchased for us. "Jesus said to the people who believed in him, 'You are truly my disciples if you keep obeying my teachings. And you will know the truth, and the truth will set you free. . . . So if the Son sets you free, you will indeed be free.'"[4]

I've learned that focusing on myself keeps me from focusing on the Lord. So in his invitation to follow, Jesus immediately addresses the need to "turn from your selfish ways." Other translations tell us to deny ourselves. To deny means to refuse, reject, veto, say no to ourselves. Every time the *self* rises to defend, promote, and impress, we are to lay it aside, reject its cry, veto its vote. If I turn from something, I remove the possibility that it will get in my way. The Lord knows that the first commitment in following him has to be our willingness to deal sternly with the old nature that wars against our desire for true life. His words are, "*You* must turn from your selfish ways" (emphasis added).

I like the apostle Paul's advice to "throw off" the old self:

Since you have heard all about him and have learned
the truth that is in Jesus, throw off your old evil
nature and your former way of life, which is rotten
through and through, full of lust and deception.
Instead, there must be a spiritual renewal of your
thoughts and attitudes. You must display a new
nature because you are a new person, created in
God's likeness—righteous, holy, and true.[5]

In order to have this spiritual renewal and new nature,
Paul gives this picture of how he died to self:

My old self has been crucified with Christ. It is no
longer I who live, but Christ lives in me. So I live in
this earthly body by trusting in the Son of God, who
loved me and gave himself for me.[6]

This is living wisely! Voices around us protest: "No, you
can't resign from your ministry." "No, you can't sell your veterinary practice." "No, you can't give up control of your life.
It doesn't make sense!" It really doesn't make sense because
life with Jesus shows us a different way: "If you try to keep
your life for yourself, you will lose it. But if you give up your
life for me, you will find true life. And how do you benefit
if you gain the whole world but lose or forfeit your own soul
in the process?"[7]

What I've learned is that dying to self offers freedom from self-seeking, self-righteousness, and self-protection. Experience has taught me that it is extremely hard work to keep promoting myself, to please people so that I can be accepted, and to protect myself from being hurt. To constantly manipulate circumstances so that *I* am noticed, approved, and not rejected is a frustrating job, mainly because it's an impossible task. As I know only too well.

It was in the late 1980s that I began to speak. One of my first seminars almost became my last. After the seminar was over, the conference committee received negative comments about me: "She's too serious." "I liked the speaker we had last year." When the committee shared the evaluations with me, I was devastated. When I was alone, I told the Lord that I would never speak again. Here was my *self* exposed, needing approval, and depressed because I was rejected. I wanted to go home, stay in my room, and feel sorry for myself.

As painful as this experience was, I learned that speaking was included on the path the Lord had for me. God knew that I needed to die to my strong bent to want to please people. I finally faced the truth that I needed to learn to accept others' opinions and not be destroyed in the process. I needed to know that my speaking was not about me; it was about God and being faithful to his truth. I needed to turn from my selfish ways and self-absorption. At one point in my frequent struggle to die to my self, I penned these words:

*"Don't lay me aside!" the old self cried.*
*"My place is not with the crucified.*
*I have my rights, you see,*
*to protect and fight for all that is ME!"*

I began to understand that even though I had initially turned over the steering wheel of my life to God, I still needed to surrender my life every day, hour by hour. I think that is why we are asked to take up our cross *daily*.

The moment of truth after the seminar was a turning point for me. It was the day that I chose freedom from my self—again. I had not fully realized how the old self drove me to be accepted by people, to be noticed and applauded, to succeed mainly for the recognition that success provides. In his wisdom and mercy, God provided the perfect circumstance for me to experience the life-giving freedom from self. Suddenly, I was much freer to serve him.

The lovely queen Esther knew what it was like to lay aside herself and trust God with her life. Raised by her uncle Mordecai, Esther, a Jewess, was chosen in a beauty contest to be the wife of King Xerxes. Her husband didn't know of her nationality, however. One day, Haman, a powerful official in the king's court, convinced the king to sign an edict that would murder all the Jews in the empire. Stunned by the news, Mordecai sent word to Esther that she must intercede for her people and plead for mercy before her husband, the king.

The problem Esther faced was that she could not have

an audience with the king unless he invited her. The rule of the court was that if she—or anyone—appeared uninvited, the king could either extend his scepter and let her approach or have her killed immediately. Interaction with the king depended entirely on his mood. Esther was hesitant to present herself to the king, but Mordecai relayed this message to encourage her: "Who knows? Maybe you were made queen for just such a time as this."[8]

Esther then asked her uncle to have the Jews fast for three days, just as she and her maidens planned to do. The queen's words to Mordecai reflected her willingness to deny herself: "And then, though it is against the law, I will go in to see the king. If I must die, I am willing to die."[9] Esther's words are an incredible articulation of the freedom she had in denying herself. She was a courageous woman who chose to live wisely.[10]

In her own way, Esther exemplified a truth expressed by the apostle Paul to the Romans:

> We don't live for ourselves or die for ourselves. If we live, it's to honor the Lord. And if we die, it's to honor the Lord. So whether we live or die, we belong to the Lord. Christ died and rose again for this very purpose—to be Lord both of the living and of the dead.[11]

These verses have helped me immensely in understanding my ability to be free from my self. The passage states that I, as a believer in Christ, belong to the Lord. God created me, died for me, and adopted me into his family. My life is the Lord's. So it is right and natural to surrender my life to him. I belong to God, not to myself.

This truth took on practical dimensions during a flight I took to Philadelphia. Because of a storm moving through the area, the plane was unable to land, so it began circling the city. If you've ever circled an airport, you can begin to appreciate how anxious the passengers on this flight became. People started to think about the consequences of arriving late and the potential of missing connections to other flights. The tension was very apparent.

The man seated to my left was consumed with frustration. Each time the pilot announced that we still had not received permission to land, the man renewed his angry outbursts: "I'm going to be late for my appointment! I'll be stuck in rush-hour traffic! I'm never flying this airline again!" As distraught and agitated as he became, the man seated to my right grew increasingly pale, quiet, and withdrawn—and eventually sick.

As I considered my own response while sitting between these two men, one angry and one ill, I realized this situation illustrated the options we have when we find ourselves in trying circumstances. One response to the obstacles in our path is to become irritated and upset with God and everyone around us. Life is not turning out the way we want, and we feel justified in our anger. The old self demands this.

A second option is to allow ourselves to become so

overwhelmed by circumstances that we succumb to events with a sense of futility and resignation. We can allow people or situations to so dominate our lives that we subconsciously withdraw from life—even to the point of physical or emotional illness. We give up on making choices and essentially limp through life without joy or hope.

While on that plane, I knew that getting angry about the situation would neither solve the problem nor help me deal with it. And I certainly didn't want to sit there and grow weak and miserable. So I prayed, *Lord, many years ago I surrendered control of my life to you. It is no longer mine; it is yours. I have the choice to be free of my self so that my responses honor you. So, Lord, if it pleases you to have me circle Philadelphia, then it pleases me.*

I have prayed this prayer in a multitude of situations and under a variety of conditions—especially those over which I have no control. Surrender is a choice I continually make to be free from my self and to rise above my circumstances.

Sometimes it is quite hard to pray, "Lord, if it pleases you for me to go through this trial, then it pleases me." Judy has not been able to have children. She is in her early thirties, and all of her close friends have two or more children. Judy and her husband have prayed, cried, and tried numerous fertility drugs and procedures. They are still hopeful, still trusting God, but they are also still contending with their feelings.

Another young woman had a "problem" that was just the opposite of Judy's. This young woman, whose name was Mary, had a surprise pregnancy. The angel Gabriel appeared to her and announced that she was to give birth to a child who would be called the Son of God. After the angel answered Mary's question about how she, who was a virgin, could have a baby, she responded, "I am the Lord's servant, and I am willing to accept whatever he wants. May everything you have said come true."[12] Mary chose to be free from self yet free to God—"I am willing to accept whatever he wants."

I love Gabriel's words to Mary: "Don't be frightened, Mary . . . for God has decided to bless you!"[13] Perhaps God chose to bless Mary, Robertson McQuilkin, and Queen Esther because he knew that their lives were his. They chose freedom from self—and each one found that it was a wise and blessed way to live.

*After surrender—what? The whole of the life after surrender is an aspiration for unbroken communion with God.*

OSWALD CHAMBERS, *My Utmost for His Highest*

# A Prayer for Wisdom

O Lord, forgive my self-absorption and desire to be in control of my life. I know I have a choice: I can wallow in self-pity because I don't get my own way or I can choose to turn from my selfish ways and live humbly in the power of your Spirit. Thank you for your sacrifice, which is a continual reminder of your love for me and the freedom the Cross gives me to lay aside the old self and to become who you want me to be—my true self that seeks to live wisely. In Jesus' name, amen.

# Reflections on the Truth

1.  Even though we have the Holy Spirit to empower us, the old self dies hard. What do you consider to be your greatest challenge in dying to self?

2.  One of the blessings of knowing Christ is that we are no longer in bondage to self. What do these verses teach about this freedom?

    a.  Romans 6:6-8

    b.  Romans 8:1-2

    c.  Galatians 5:16

3.  Instead of being slaves to our sinful nature, we are free to follow the Holy Spirit. How do the following verses explain the work of the Spirit in our lives?

    a.  John 16:13-14

    b.  Romans 8:26-27

    c.  Galatians 5:22-26

4. Spend some time meditating on the Phillips translation of Galatians 2:20, either by reading it aloud, writing it down, memorizing it, or rewriting it as your own personal prayer:

> I died on the cross with Christ. And my present life is not that of the old "I", but the living Christ within me. The bodily life I now live, I live believing in the Son of God, who loved me and sacrificed himself for me.

# Scripture to Believe

[Jesus said,] "If you try to hang on to your life, you will lose it. But if you give up your life for my sake, you will save it."

LUKE 9:24

FIVE

# KEEP YOUR HAND IN HIS

*I have found safety and security in a loving heavenly Father,*
*who cannot be shaken, who will never leave me or forsake me,*
*and in whom I can trust completely. For those looking for hope,*
*I recommend grabbing the hand of your heavenly Father as*
*tightly as possible, like a little child does with his parent.*

LISA BEAMER, *Let's Roll!*


*For I hold you by your right hand—*
  *I, the LORD your God.*
  *And I say to you,*
  *"Don't be afraid. I am here to help you."*

ISAIAH 41:13

I CLOSE ALL MY CORRESPONDENCE with the words *Keep your hand in his.* When saying good-bye to friends, I usually share these parting words: "Keep your hand in his." This one truth, above all others, has been the cornerstone of my life. I can believe that God is right, that he is for me, that he is trust-worthy, but until I surrender and choose to take hold of his hand and walk with him, I will never know him intimately. As Oswald Chambers encourages us, "The whole of the life after surrender is an aspiration for unbroken communion with God."[1] Seeking this unbroken communion with the Lord has kept me on the narrow path and continually equips me to live wisely in Christ.

Because I believe that a growing intimacy with God is crucial in experiencing all he has for us, I often speak about abiding in Christ. I define *abiding* as consistently sitting at the feet of Jesus, listening to his words with a heart to obey. Abiding in Jesus is spending time alone with him, reading his Word, and praying. My shortened definition is "keeping your hand in his."

During a question-and-answer time at a seminar, I inter-acted with a young woman who typifies the struggle most of us have in keeping our hands in the Lord's. In a previous session, I had shared my thoughts about Mary and Martha, the two sisters whom Jesus often visited. Each woman had a different kind of relationship with him. When Jesus and his disciples came to their home in Bethany, Mary immediately went with the Lord, sat at his feet, and listened to his words;

Martha immediately went into the kitchen to prepare a meal for them. Mary sat still; Martha busily served.

In the earlier session, I had read aloud the Scripture passage that relates the conversation Jesus and Martha had about what Mary was "doing"—or, from Martha's perspective, what her sister was *not* doing. Martha anxiously approached Jesus and said, "Lord, doesn't it seem unfair to you that my sister just sits here while I do all the work? Tell her to come and help me."[2] Jesus replied, "My dear Martha, you are worried and upset over all these details! There is only one thing worth being concerned about. Mary has discovered it, and it will not be taken away from her."[3]

I spent the majority of my presentation emphasizing that Jesus said only one thing is worth being concerned about: sitting at his feet and listening to his words. I concluded by saying that it is so easy to be distracted by serving the Lord and others that we allow these good things to crowd out our time with the Lord. Jesus loved both of these dear sisters, but he was quite clear that Mary had chosen the *one* thing that was necessary—and he wasn't going to ask her to give it up to help Martha.

So, at the question-and-answer time, the young woman said to me, "I am a Martha, and I will always be a Martha. I have three children, and I serve in several areas in our church. I like being busy. I don't like being still, and besides that, I never have time to be quiet and read anything, much less the Bible. I've tried it, and it doesn't work for me. This is who I am, and I can't change. And what about single moms who never have any time, or women who work full-time?"

For this "Martha," it was almost unreasonable to think that someone would take time or *have* time to spend with God. In our busy, program-driven, activity-oriented world, we tend to view taking time to be still, to hear from God, as a luxury or an impossibility.

We face demands on our time from every aspect of our lives: family, friends, work, church, and community. These are good, legitimate demands, but ones that nevertheless keep us from the one thing we need to be concerned about. Contemplation, silence, and quietness are rare commodities. Consistent, unhurried times with God are not the norm for most of us. Most often, it's not because we don't want to have that time with the Lord; it's just that the day somehow gets away from us. We make New Year's resolutions to read through the Bible or to have daily times with God, but by February or March, we've fallen behind. We get discouraged and give up trying. It does sound like an almost unobtainable goal to think that we can consistently sit at the feet of Jesus.

The irony of this dilemma is that the very activity that gives strength to the tired, refreshment to the worn out, and perspective to those who are burned out is the one thing that is most easy to neglect. In Matthew 11:28, Jesus extends this gracious invitation: "Come to me, all of you who are weary and carry heavy burdens, and I will give you rest." Jesus offers to to take hold of our hand, walk with us, and teach us to live wisely in this pressure-filled world.

I remember the first time I clearly heard the Lord's invitation to place my hand in his. It was at one of the busiest, most hectic times in my life. I was a young mother with three small children, and Jack was very busy with his veterinary practice. I had tried living the Christian life in the only way I knew how—by regular church attendance and sporadic Bible study and prayer—but something was missing. I was tired and weary. As I pondered the Lord's invitation to come to him, I realized that what God wanted was a personal, intimate relationship with me. This was not a requirement, a command, or a duty—it was a loving offer to bless me, strengthen me, and teach me. For that to happen, though, I needed to place my hand in his and make myself available to learn from him. I knew that I would need to be intentional, but I was ready for a profound lifestyle change.

The problem I faced was that my circumstances were unchangeable. I still had a busy husband, active young children who demanded my attention, numerous pets, and an old house that needed lots of attention. My days were filled with the kinds of activities that all young mothers face: caring for the children, shopping, cooking, cleaning, laundry, answering the phone. I felt as if I had all I could do just to stay clothed and in my right mind. I laughed one time when someone asked what my hobbies were. Who had time for hobbies?

But in the midst of all that busyness, I wanted to take time to sit at the feet of Jesus. I tried getting up before the children and reading the Bible, but, as one mother put it, "My children wake up at the first crack of the Bible." I tried reading the Bible and having a quiet time before I went to bed, but I was always too tired and would fall asleep.

As I prayed about how I would read the Bible and pray somewhat consistently, I realized that I could memorize Scripture. I wrote verses on index cards and placed them over the diaper-changing table and over the kitchen sink, as well as over the bathroom sink. These were places where I spent a lot of time, and while I was there, I could also read, memorize, and meditate on his Word throughout the day. I chose verses that I needed—especially ones about patience and trust.

I invited a couple of friends from church to come to my home for coffee and Bible study once a week. Knowing that I would be meeting with others motivated me to make time to study. Then, as often as I could, I made the hour after lunch a quiet time for the children—and especially for me. While the children either slept or played quietly, I could read, pray, and be still. This is how I began to keep my hand in the Lord's.

In answer to the young woman's question about how single moms and women who work long hours in or outside the home can ever find time to be still, I have good news and bad news. The bad news is that no matter what your situation or season of life might be, it is always an uphill battle to spend time with God. Now that my children have left home, I'm still prone to let other seemingly urgent demands interfere with my time with the Lord. Jesus knew about busyness, and he warned that "all too quickly the message is crowded out by the cares of this life."[4]

The good news is that it is possible to live in this truth: You can keep your hand in his. If you earnestly desire to grow in your relationship with the Lord and if you are willing to be flexible, you can abide in Christ. Let me share with you how I've learned in the past few years to keep my hand in his.

One day, when I was reading Oswald Chambers's *My Utmost for His Highest*, I was struck by his insight about a rather easily overlooked verse in Genesis: "After that, Abram traveled southward and set up camp in the hill country between Bethel on the west and Ai on the east. There he built an altar and worshiped the LORD."[5] Chambers writes, "Bethel is the symbol of communion with God; Ai is the symbol of the world. Abraham pitched his tent between the two. The measure of the worth of our public activity for God is the private profound communion we have with Him. Rush is wrong every time; there is always plenty of time to worship God. Quiet days with God may be a snare. We have to pitch our tents where we shall always have quiet times with God, however noisy our times with the world may be."[6]

As I meditated on these thoughts, I concluded that I needed a tent! Since my journey usually takes me into Ai (the world) or to Bethel (which literally means "house of God"),[7] I realized that I needed to pitch my tent (spend time with God) between the world and my times in church. Because I was in church only once or twice a week, I knew that if I wanted to keep my hand in God's, I needed to spend time alone with him, one-on-one, every day. In order to do this, I found a "tent" and put my "altar" in it. My tent is a cloth bag in which I have placed my altar: my Bible, a journal, and a devotional book. I usually include a Bible study book or a current book that I am reading. A tent can be a special bag, a backpack, or a briefcase—anything that is portable and can be taken with you whenever you leave your home.

My tent stays near my chair in my study, and it's ready to be pitched early in the morning. But if circumstances keep me from spending time with the Lord at the beginning of the day, I pick up my tent and take it with me when I leave the house. (In fact, I take it with me even if I already have had time with the Lord.) Then throughout the day, I look for pockets of time when I can pitch my tent—unplanned times of waiting or having a few extra minutes before a commit- ment. I can set up my tent in an airport, a doctor's waiting room, a coffee shop, a library, a park. If you work outside your home, it is helpful to have your tent available so that you can pitch it during a coffee break, lunch, or in your office or car before you drive home. I have found that I am much more consistent in spending time with the Lord because I always have my tent with me.

Certainly, I prefer starting the day with the Lord, but I've found that's not always possible. For many years, I thought that time with God could take place only when everything was quiet, but as Oswald Chambers said, "Quiet days with God may be a snare." The snare was my thinking that if I missed the early-morning quiet time, then I would have to wait until the next morning to spend time with God. It has been freeing to have my tent ready to pitch whenever I can find a few moments to myself in the midst of a busy world. Chambers reminds us that "we have to pitch our tents where we shall always have quiet times with God, however noisy our times with the world may be."

The blessing of always having my tent with me is that I can be more consistent and creative in when I spend time with God. It's not a ritual, and it's not bound by the parameters of time or place. Sometimes I have only fifteen minutes, but often I am able to spend more time than I expected. I've found over the years that consistency is more important than the length of time I spend with the Lord. Anytime I stop and intently read his Word with an obedient heart, I find that the Scriptures are "full of living power . . . sharper than the sharpest knife, cutting deep into our innermost thoughts and desires."[8] I need the cutting edge of the Scriptures daily, and I have found that any amount of time I spend reading the Word is always profitable.

When I keep my hand in his, my conversation with the Lord—prayer—is natural and continual. In reality, it is only through consistent abiding that I can have an effective prayer life. Jesus taught, "If you stay joined to me and my words remain in you, you may ask any request you like, and it will be granted!"[9] I think that Jesus could make this promise because he knows that if I am growing in intimacy with him and treasuring his Word, then my prayers are concerned more about what's on *his* heart than about what's on mine. My requests are directed more toward the eternal than the temporal, more toward the accomplishing of his will in the world than toward the pleasure I seek in mine.

Choosing to stay connected to the Lord is my way of acknowledging my need for wisdom in living in this unpredictable world. I admit that apart from Christ, my feeble attempts to love, to be patient, to be self-controlled are futile. My walking with the Lord allows him to teach and guide me daily. As I pitch my tent, he prompts me to call a friend, write a note, or ask for forgiveness. Keeping company with the Lord enables me to wrestle with him over the inequities and uncertainties I encounter. Because my hand is firmly planted in his, I am assured of his presence when I walk through the trials of the day or the deep waters of suffering.

Keeping my hand in his has also allowed the Lord to superintend my "busyness." One time, I committed myself to reading to children enrolled in the Head Start program. God gently but firmly spoke to my heart and said, *Cynthia, there will be a season in your life when it will be appropriate for you to read to these children, but for now, I think it's best that you stay home and read to your own children.* I would not have heard these thoughts if I had not placed my hand in his and begun to sit at his feet. The best thing I can do for my family is to walk with God. The best thing I can do for my church is to consistently pitch my tent. The very best thing I can do for myself is to keep my hand in his. (This is especially true and necessary for single moms.)

It's not a choice between *sitting* (Mary) or *serving* (Martha). For me, the *sitting* is a prerequisite to knowing the *serving* that is God-directed, that furthers his Kingdom, and that is right for me. Personally, I feel that when the Lord says, "There is really only one thing worth being concerned about," we need to listen seriously to what he says. Maybe God is right after all!

Keeping our hands in his makes it possible to choose the good part, to rest, to have some semblance of balance in our lives, and to receive his help. Abiding in Christ empowers us to live wisely.

*What does it mean to abide in Him? I think it means three things: First, a* conscious awareness of His presence *at all times. That does not mean direct verbal communication with Him, but the feeling that He is there.
. . . Second, it also means a* careful consultation with Him *about everything that affects us. That consultation may be in direct prayer, or else in scanning the Bible indirectly for any message He has for us there. . . . Third, it means a* continual enjoyment of Him as a person. *That means He is a joy, a delight to us at all times; the very thought of Him fills us with pleasure.*[10]

W. GLYN EVANS

# A Prayer for Wisdom

Heavenly Father, there really is only one thing to be concerned about. Thank you for making this clear. I'm blessed by your invitation to walk with you, to learn from you, and to keep company with you. I don't have to strive to find you or just hope that you are with me when I come to sit in your presence. You invite, you call, you wait for me to come to you. You are always available to meet with me. I am the one so easily distracted, too busy to pitch my tent.

That's why I like the thought of placing my hand in yours each day and walking with you throughout my journey. When I do this, I am aware of your presence in my life. You are readily available to answer my questions, calm my fears, and guide me. I want to grow in your grace and knowledge. I don't want to walk through this world alone or come to the end of my life realizing I never took time to know you and to experience the freedom and rest that only you can give. I want to keep my hand in yours. Thank you for always reaching out for mine. In Jesus' name, amen.

# Reflections on the Truth

1. God desires intimacy with you. What do the following verses reveal about how God will help you stay close to him?

   a. Psalm 63:8

   b. Matthew 11:28-30

   c. John 15:5

2. James 4:8 affirms: "Draw close to God, and God will draw close to you."[11]

   a. How would you describe your abiding in Christ—your drawing close to him?

   b. In what ways do you experience God drawing close to you?

3. Jesus taught that the cares of this life, the deceitfulness of riches, and the desire for other things can crowd out the Word and make its reception unfruitful.[12] In what way(s) can you identify with this caution from the Lord? What can be changed in your life so that you can spend more time with God?

4. Psalm 84:10 sums up the joy of abiding: "A single day in your courts is better than a thousand anywhere else!" Write a prayer of thanksgiving to God for the blessings of spending time in his "courts."

# Scripture to Believe

I follow close behind you; your strong right hand
holds me securely.

PSALM 63:8, NLT-1996

# GOD'S WORD IS ALL THE TRUTH YOU'LL EVER NEED

*Every year I live—in fact, nearly every day—I seem to see more clearly how all the peace, happiness, and power of the Christian life hinges on one thing. That one thing is taking God at His word, believing He really means exactly what He says, and accepting the very words that reveal His goodness and grace . . .*

FRANES RIDLEY HAVERGAL, quoted in *Streams in the Desert*, March 24

*All Scripture is inspired by God and is useful to teach us what is true and to make us realize what is wrong in our lives. It corrects us when we are wrong and teaches us to do what is right. God uses it to prepare and equip his people to do every good work.*

2 TIMOTHY 3:16-17

AMY CARMICHAEL SPENT HER LIFE rescuing girls from slavery and prostitution in India. Although she was committed to serving the Lord, she, like any young woman, desired to be married. But because her work with the Dohnavur Fellowship, the mission she established to care for the rescued girls, was so demanding, Amy realized she might never marry. As she wrestled with this possibility, Amy knew she needed to hear from God. So she took time to sit at his feet and listen to his Word.

Forty years later, she shared that experience with a young woman who was also facing the prospect of living a life of singleness. Amy wrote, "On this day many years ago, I went away alone to a cave in the mountain called Arima. I had feelings of fear about the future. That is why I went there—to be alone with God. The devil kept on whispering, 'It's all right now, but what about afterward? You are going to be very lonely.' And he painted pictures of loneliness—I can see them still. And I turned to my God in a kind of desperation and said, 'Lord, what can I do? How can I go on to the end?' And He said, 'None of them that trust in [Me] shall be desolate.'¹ That word has been with me ever since."² For Amy, this word from God assured her, sustained her, and comforted her. It was all the truth she needed to stay on the true and right path.

I've also had experiences in which God's Word had guided me through my struggles. Early in our marriage, Jack felt it was time for him to establish his own veterinary practice. We could move anywhere, so we asked God to lead us to the place he wanted us to live. As we looked at various options, I had my checklist of questions: What size town was it? What were the schools like? What social and cultural opportunities would be available? What were the churches like? What about the climate? How close would we be to family?

But in the course of my Bible reading and study, I found a passage that pierced my heart with conviction. "Trust in the LORD with all your heart, and do not rely on your own insight. In all your ways acknowledge him, and he will make straight your paths."3 There it was, a simple, profound, practical truth—truth that made sense, spoke to my need, and offered peace and freedom. Since that time, I have come to appreciate the way Eugene Peterson paraphrased it: "Trust GOD from the bottom of your heart; don't try to figure out everything on your own. Listen for GOD's voice in everything you do, everywhere you go; he's the one who will keep you on track."4

How liberating this truth is. We don't have to try to figure out everything on our own. We don't have to be anxious. We can be at peace because if we wholeheartedly trust God and truly listen for his voice, he will keep us on track. He will show us the way. I had chosen the road less traveled, and this verse showed me how I could stay on that road to a new place. I had simply to trust God and follow his leading.

Trusting that God's Word is all the truth we'll ever need

flies in the face of the wisdom of our culture. People ask, "How can you base your life on the Bible? The Bible is full of inconsistencies and was written thousands of years ago. It doesn't speak to our contemporary culture."

Beth, the daughter of a friend, came to me with some of these very same thoughts. "Cynthia, I don't understand the Bible, and I'm not even sure that I believe everything in it. Will you help me?"

As I began to meet with Beth, I shared with her the apostle Paul's observation: "People who aren't Christians can't understand these truths from God's Spirit. It all sounds foolish to them because only those who have the Spirit can understand what the Spirit means."[5]

I told her that the key to embracing the truth of the Scriptures is a personal relationship with Jesus Christ. When we accept Christ's finished work on the cross, acknowledge our sin, and ask him to be our Savior and Lord, then the Holy Spirit indwells us and begins to teach and guide us into all truth.

Beth persisted with her questions. "But, Cynthia, how do we know the Bible is really *God*'s Word? After all, lots of people wrote the books of the Bible, and they wrote them thousands of years ago. How do we know the Bible is really from God?"

I read her what the apostle Peter wrote: "Above all, you must realize that no prophecy in Scripture ever came from the prophet's own understanding, or from human initiative. No, those prophets were moved by the Holy Spirit, and they spoke from God."[6] Because the Holy Spirit authored the Word of God and because the Spirit lives within us, he is the one who authenticates the truth to each person. I've heard the Bible described as "the only book in the world that when you open it up, the author shows up!"

As Beth acknowledged her belief in Christ, asking the Holy Spirit to teach and guide her, she began to accept the authority and sufficiency of the Word of God. I explained to her, "It's not that we don't seek other truth apart from the Bible; it's that whatever truth we discover, we measure by God's Word. Many excellent books help us understand the truth in the Scriptures and the truth about ourselves. But we should recognize that the origin of all truth is in the Bible, and if some idea can't be supported by Scripture, then perhaps we need to examine it carefully."

Beth would frequently ask me what I thought about various issues she faced in life, and I would reply, "Beth, it is not what *I* think. What's important is what the *Bible* says."

One day she said to me, "What do you think about a wife needing to submit to her husband? Is that right?"

I responded by saying, "The Scriptures are clear that wives are to submit to our husbands as to the Lord."[7] I went on to explain: "Because God created us and the institution of marriage, then perhaps his instructions for how this special relationship works should be taken to heart. Since I gave my life to Christ, my desire has been to please and obey him. Throughout fifty-five years of marriage, I have discovered that for me, submission is voluntarily giving up my desire to control my husband. It is loving him more than I love myself, and it is trusting God to guide Jack and me on the best path.

"I'm not a doormat; I share my thoughts and opinions, and we have hearty discussions about decisions that need to be made. These discussions usually end with both of us agreeing on what should be done. But on the few occasions when giving up my agenda is needful, I choose to submit because I desire to obey God and to honor and respect my husband. Let me add that Ephesians 5:22 makes it clear that our submission is 'as to the Lord'—that it is biblical and it never condones abuse of any kind. It means that we would never consent to anything that is not in keeping with God's commands."

Wayne Grudem, a professor of biblical and systematic theology, discusses a declaration Jesus made when he prayed to his Father on behalf of his disciples: "Sanctify them by the truth; your word is truth."[8] Grudem makes these observations:

> This verse is interesting because Jesus does not use the adjectives *alēthinos* or *alēthēs* ("true"), which we might have expected, to say, "Your word is true." Rather, he uses a noun, *alētheia* ("truth"), to say that God's Word is not simply "true," but it is truth itself.
>
> The difference is significant, for this statement encourages us to think of the Bible not simply as being "true" in the sense that it conforms to some higher standard of truth, but rather to think of the

Bible as being itself the final standard of truth. The Bible is God's Word, and God's Word is the ultimate definition of what is true and what is not true: God's Word is itself *truth*. Thus we are to think of the Bible as the ultimate standard of truth, the reference point by which every other claim to truthfulness is to be measured.[9]

The Scriptures themselves confirm Grudem's statement. In Paul's letter to the Ephesians, he writes that when we grow in our faith, truth serves as an anchor in our lives. "Then we will no longer be like children, forever changing our minds about what we believe because someone has told us something different or because someone has cleverly lied to us and made the lie sound like the truth. Instead, we will hold to the truth in love, becoming more and more in every way like Christ, who is the head of his body, the church."[10]

It does take faith to believe that the Bible is truth, but when we do, we find a living, active Word that addresses the essential issues of life and enables us to live wisely. One of the New Testament writers describes the Scriptures this way: "The word of God is full of living power. It is sharper than the sharpest knife, cutting deep into our innermost thoughts and desires. It exposes us for what we really are."[11] The Word does cut to the quick and work in our hearts, prompting us to forgive, to love, to trust, to obey.

Peter and Maria had been living together for several months when they first attended a Los Angeles church. Going to church was new for them. They liked the music and the energy, so they returned. They heard about the importance of surrendering their lives to Jesus, so they did. Unreservedly.

The pastor preached from the Bible, which they knew little about. Curious about what else the Bible had to say, they bought one and started to read it. One day, while reading the New Testament, Maria read these words from 1 Corinthians 6: "Run from sexual sin! No other sin so clearly affects the body as this one does. For sexual immorality is a sin against your own body. Don't you realize that your body is the temple of the Holy Spirit, who lives in you and was given to you by God? You do not belong to yourself, for God bought you with a high price. So you must honor God with your body."[12] The words disturbed her. Her body was the temple of the Holy Spirit? Sex with Peter was a sin against her own body? What was that all about? She had never read anything like that before. What did it mean for her life?

Because Maria wanted to follow Jesus, she took the words of Scripture seriously. "Peter, we can't sleep together anymore. The Bible says so. We've got to stop this." After Maria and Peter talked about the words from the Bible, they decided that until they were married, they would not have sex. In fact, they wouldn't even live in the same apartment.[13]

What I find so amazing about this story is that Maria and Peter had not attended any classes in which the teacher said that sleeping together was wrong. The church leaders had not come to them to say, "We hear the two of you are living together. If you say you are Christians, you won't do that anymore." God's Word was all the truth they needed to convict them to make a change and do the right thing.

The truth of God's Word showed Peter and Maria what was wrong in their lives. It straightened them out and taught them to do what is right. The Bible shows us the right path and teaches us to prize and embrace wisdom.

When Martin and Gracia Burnham were serving as missionaries in the Philippines, they were captured by the Abu Sayyaf terrorists. For a harrowing year, the Burnhams were dragged from place to place, not knowing what would happen to them. In the end, Martin lost his life. At one point in their captivity, Martin reminded Gracia about the teachings of God's Word: "Jesus said that if you want to be great in God's kingdom, be the servant of all. And when he said 'all,' he meant all. He didn't say be the servant of everyone but terrorists. Jesus also said to love your enemies. Do good to those who hate you. Pray for those who despitefully use you and persecute you."[14]

The truth of God's Word was what Martin and Gracia needed. "That's what we started doing—praying for our captors, who were despitefully using us," Gracia writes.[15] It was the truth found in the Bible that helped Martin and Gracia live in the presence of their enemies.

Mel Birdwell, whose husband, Brian, was seriously burned in the 9/11 attack on the Pentagon, testified to God's love and presence during this trial. In *Refined by Fire*, Brian wrote of the comfort and ministry of the Word in his life during his lengthy recovery process. He describes his wife's faithfulness in ministering to him by reading the Bible: "Mel continually stood by my bed and read the Psalms and other passages of Scripture to me. Hearing words from the Bible had become even more important to me in such a time of emotional and physical pain. I wanted Mel to read to me as much as she could. It seemed as if every psalm she read talked about God carrying me in his right hand and protecting me. I felt God was talking directly to us. Through the Bible he was telling us that he protected me from my enemies and that justice would be his. It was comforting and powerful to hear her read, to be reminded of the great God we serve."[16]

My friend Emily also learned the trustworthiness of God's Word during a recent time of distress. She remembers the day nine years ago when she and her older sister, Callie, accompanied their mother to a doctor's visit. "Sarah," the doctor said to her mother, "I'm afraid I have bad news. The biopsy showed cancer cells. We are going to have to do surgery." Callie sucked in her breath. It was three months to the day that she had heard the same news from *her* physician. The terry-cloth turban wrapped around Callie's hairless head was a mute testament to her recent chemotherapy treatments.

After the doctor explained several things to the mother, he turned to Emily. "I hear you have an immune-system dysfunction. I don't want to scare you, but what has happened to your mom and your sister makes you a target. A very large target. Be sure you have frequent mammograms and do monthly self-checks."

For eight years Emily breathed a sigh of relief and thanked God when the mammogram results were normal. Then came the ninth year. The radiologist announced, "We see some abnormal cells, and we want to schedule a biopsy." Emily was stunned. Would this be the year she would learn that her immune system could not fend off the cancer cells?

As Emily walked through the days of uncertainty, she began to worry. For months before the abnormal tests, a relapse of her chronic immune-system illness had left her running on empty. Her mind raced: *How will I cope? What effect will cancer and chemotherapy have on my family? Where will I get the strength?*

In answer to her question, she was reminded of the words of Scripture: "Don't worry about anything; instead, pray about everything. Tell God what you need, and thank him for all he has done. Then you will experience God's peace, which exceeds anything we can understand."[17] She knew those were God's instructions to her: Don't worry, just pray and tell me what you need. She also knew that they were not suggestions; they were a command.

So began a discipline. When the inevitable worries invaded Emily's heart and mind, she chose to trust the truth of God's Word. She told herself, *I won't go there. I will not use my energy worrying. I have prayed about this situation. I believe my life is in God's hands and that he is good. I won't do it.* She confronted her worries with the truth of Scripture. And as she did, an incredible peace filled her life.

The morning she was to hear the biopsy results, she awoke feeling optimistic. When her friend Carol called, she told her: "I'm not at all anxious. You know me well enough to know that's God, not me. His Word told me not to worry, and I'm not. My hope is not in the results of the test. My hope is in God."

Later that day, Emily learned that the cells were not cancerous. When I talked with her, she said, "I'm relieved to know I don't have cancer, but I am even more grateful to know without a doubt that God's Word is true! The Scriptures, as nothing else could, met my need in a powerful way. It was just what I needed."

Emily would agree with Jesus' teaching in the Sermon on the Mount:

> Anyone who listens to my teaching and follows
> it is wise, like a person who builds a house on
> solid rock. Though the rain comes in torrents and
> the floodwaters rise and the winds beat against
> that house, it won't collapse because it is built on
> bedrock.[18]

Certainly, obeying God's Word equips us to live wisely, for it is all sufficient.

> *Get wisdom; develop good judgment.*
> *Don't forget my words or turn away from them.*
> *Don't turn your back on wisdom, for she will protect you.*
> *Love her, and she will guard you.*

PROVERBS 4:5-6

# A Prayer for Wisdom

May I allow the Scriptures to show me truth, correct my mistakes, and train me to live your way. Let me not be satisfied with only hearing the Word, but let me have a heart ready to obey.

Thank you for preserving your Word throughout the centuries and for the sufficiency of your Word for all my needs. My prayer is that I will honor it by letting it be the one book I cling to, turn to, and cherish for the rest of my life. In Jesus' name, amen.

# Reflections on the Truth

1.  Psalm 1 is a brief tribute to those who delight in the Lord and his Word. Read the first three verses, and describe the person who values God's Word (his law).

2.  Just about every verse in Psalm 119 extols the Word of God. Write out the benefits of the Word as expressed in the following verses:

    a. Psalm 119:11

    b. Psalm 119:50

    c. Psalm 119:98

    d. Psalm 119:105

    e. Psalm 119:114

3. God's Word is not just a book; it is his inspired Word alive and full of living power. Briefly describe the place the Bible holds in your life.

## Scripture to Believe

All Scripture is inspired by God and is useful to teach us what is true and to make us realize what is wrong in our lives. It corrects us when we are wrong and teaches us to do what is right. God uses it to prepare and equip his people to do every good work.

2 TIMOTHY 3:16-17

# YOU WILL NEVER REGRET
# DOING WHAT IS RIGHT

*True righteousness means being like God, not simply obeying him.*

LAWRENCE O. RICHARDS, *New International Encyclopedia of Bible Words*

*Since we know that God is always right, we also know that all who do what is right are his children.*

I JOHN 2:29, NLT-1996

MY HUSBAND BEFRIENDED BEN, a homeless person he met at a coffee shop. Ben had been in our home a few times and had eaten several meals with us.

One morning, Jack told me that Ben was coming over to do some yard work and might stay through lunch. I didn't have a problem with Ben's being at our home. The problem I had, though, was that we were expecting guests for lunch that day, and Ben was not on my guest list. I had planned a special lunch with flowers, cloth napkins, and a shrimp salad. I asked Jack if I could fix Ben a sandwich so that he could eat it at his convenience at the picnic table. Jack wisely said, "Well, let's see how things go."

I was a little anxious about how everything would work out. What would this older couple think of our having a homeless man around our house, especially if he ate lunch with us? How many place settings should I set at the table? Would Ben spoil our time with our special friends? Did God want me to ask Ben to join us?

All morning, the words of Jesus kept echoing in my mind: "When you put on a luncheon or a dinner . . . don't invite your friends. . . . Instead, invite the poor, the crippled, the lame, and the blind."[1]

God's Word answered my question about whether to invite Ben to join us for lunch. I went ahead and set a place for him at the table. We all enjoyed our conversation, and then Ben excused himself after eating. The lunch went well. Ben experienced the fellowship of Christians, our friends were very accepting, and I had peace because, in this situation, it was the right thing to do.

"What does it cost to be a Christian?" someone asked devotional writer and poet Henry Drummond. His reply was, "The entrance fee . . . is nothing, but the annual subscription is everything."[2] Drummond echoes the apostle Paul's words about the entrance fee: "The wages of sin is death, but the free gift of God is eternal life through Christ Jesus our Lord."[3] God's gift of eternal life is free, but the expense of the annual subscription is described in this paraphrase of the letter to the Ephesians: "Take on an entirely new way of life—a God-fashioned life, a life renewed from the inside and working itself into your conduct as God accurately reproduces his character in you."[4]

The entrance into God's Kingdom has been freely paid by Christ's death on the cross, and with this gracious gift, we receive freedom from our old nature and a new life to be lived in the likeness of our heavenly Father. The annual subscription cost is a dying to self, accompanied by a wholehearted desire to do what is right. Through Christ, the power of sin has been broken, and we now have the power to live for the glory of God. Again, the apostle Paul exhorts us:

> Do not let sin control the way you live; do not
> give in to sinful desires. . . . Instead, give yourselves
> completely to God, for you were dead, but now
> you have new life. So use your whole body as an
> instrument to do what is right for the glory of God.[5]

I saw these verses lived out by a woman I met at a weekend conference. Kay asked if we could have lunch together, and when we met the next day, she told me a compelling story. "I used to have a high-paying job at a good company. I really enjoyed what I did, and my flexible hours allowed me to be available to our teenage children. But after I had been at the company for a while, I found myself attracted to a coworker, even though my husband and I have always had a good relationship. I was extremely careful about how I related to my colleague and was confident that he was oblivious to my thoughts and feelings. I assumed the "crush" would soon pass, but I couldn't seem to control my emotions.

"I prayed, I confessed my sin, and I even told a trusted friend and asked her to pray for and with me. This helped, but as the months passed, my unrighteous thoughts continued to dominate my life. I began to feel hopeless and didn't know what to do. It was during a time of crying out to God that I felt his leading to quit my job. *Quit?* I took a deep breath. This job was the best, and we needed the money. How would I explain to everyone, especially my husband, why I was leaving such a good job?

"But the Lord was clear: 'Kay, flee from youthful lusts.' I knew that God was right, and I was so ready to end my emotional turmoil that I immediately handed in my resignation."

As I listened to Kay, I thought back to another conference, when I had listened to Suzanne's heartbreaking story of giving in to temptation, of having an affair. In the process, Suzanne lost her husband.

These two women were both enticed by their own desires, yet their responses stood in stark contrast. Suzanne, although restored and forgiven, still lives with regret for doing what was wrong. Kay, on the other hand, lives with no regret because she did what was right.

Before Kay and I finished our lunch that day, I asked her what she had told others about why she resigned so abruptly. She continued her story: "I struggled with how to answer people who asked me why I was leaving. I wanted to be truthful, but I certainly didn't want to implicate my coworker. Actually, this process was much harder than I thought it would be. I wished I could have just slipped away, but I wanted to do what was right. I realized that God was using my decision to solidify my faith and that he wanted me to share honestly about what it means to have a relationship with him. I was scared and embarrassed, but the Lord gave me wisdom.

"First, I knew that I should respond only to those who asked me why I was leaving. I didn't need to go around telling everyone. To my colleagues who asked, I said, 'I have so enjoyed working here. It has been a blessing, but I have been struggling in the past few months with some personal issues that were affecting my relationship with God. I felt that in order to honor him, I needed to make this difficult decision to leave. The bottom line is that nothing is more valuable to me than my relationship with God.'

"To my husband, I was honest. In a way, my telling him the truth brought us closer together. He understood that I was willing to sacrifice my job so that our marriage would not be compromised. His acceptance of me has deepened my love and respect for him.

"To my Christian friends, I felt that the truth would serve as a warning and a testimony that doing the right thing means we must make hard choices. Several women have thanked me for telling them about my experience. And, Cynthia, the reason I wanted to tell you my story is so that you can encourage other women who are faced with temptation. Tell them that in my case, there was a cost in doing what was right, but the cost was miniscule compared to what I would have lost. This happened several years ago, and I have never regretted my decision."

Kay's life illustrates that doing what is right is not always easy, and it often involves sacrifice. This is part of the "subscription rate" that Drummond referred to when he said that it costs everything. It does cost, but as God's child who loves and honors her Father, Kay gladly paid the price.

The Old Testament's story of Joseph is similar to Kay's. Joseph, betrayed by his jealous brothers, was sold into slavery in Egypt, where he became a valuable servant in the home of Potiphar, the captain of the pharaoh's guard. The Scriptures describe Joseph as a "handsome and well-built young man."[6] Potiphar's wife was attracted to Joseph and pressured him to sleep with her. His response was, "How could I do such a wicked thing? It would be a great sin against God."[7]

Joseph successfully avoided her until one day, when no one else was around, she became more aggressive in her seduction. She grabbed him by his robe and demanded that he satisfy her desire. Joseph tore himself away from her and left the room, but the scorned woman lied to her husband and accused Joseph of trying to rape her. As a result, Joseph was thrown into prison—a high cost to pay for running from a seductive woman who promised pleasure. Joseph could have easily rationalized his choice to stay with her. Who would have known? After all, he was living in a foreign culture.

But Joseph knew what was right and what was wrong. He knew that if he did what was wrong, it would be a great sin—not only against Potiphar and his wife but, more important, against God himself. Nothing, not even the fleeting pleasure of sex, was worth jeopardizing his relationship with God. Fully knowing that he would suffer for his refusal, Joseph chose to do what was right. Joseph spent the next few years in prison, but that experience was one in a series of events that led to his becoming the leader that saved Egypt and the nation of Israel from severe famine.[8]

The world we live in would laugh at Joseph's choice to run from Potiphar's wife: "You, of all people, deserve to have a little happiness. Besides, Joseph, she wasn't going to tell. Look where 'doing what is right' got you. It's not worth it. Why be so different?" I like what G. K. Chesterton said: "A saint is one who exaggerates what the world neglects."[9]

Why make this kind of choice? Good question, especially when our culture applauds us anytime we can beat the system. When a contractor gave my friend Lori the bill for the new addition to her home, she paid it immediately. A short time later, she became curious about the cost of the paint, so she looked over the bill more closely. To her surprise, she found that the items had not been totaled correctly. In fact, the contractor had undercharged her by $2,000. Wanting to do the right thing, Lori went to the contractor's office, explained the error, and presented a check for the correct amount. Everyone was astounded at her honesty and her commitment to doing what was right.

As Lori's story suggests, a commitment to doing what is right affects all of life. The Bible teaches us to do *everything* to the glory of God. This truth is effectively illustrated in Charles M. Sheldon's classic book *In His Steps*,[10] which tells the story of a handful of people who committed themselves to living as Christ would live in the world today. Whenever they were faced with a decision, they asked, "What would Jesus do?"

The apostle John confirmed the validity of this question by writing, "Those who say they live in God should live their lives as Jesus did."[11]

We learn to think like Jesus because he has given us a "new way of life—a God-fashioned life, a life renewed from the inside and working itself into your conduct as God accurately reproduces his character in you."[12] Kay, Joseph, and Lori all chose to do what was right and to live wisely because they willingly allowed God to reproduce his character in them.

You may ask, "But how do I know what is right?"

How did the people who asked, "What would Jesus do?" know what he would do?

First, we pray. The Bible tells us, "If you need wisdom—if you want to know what God wants you to do—ask him, and he will gladly tell you. He will not resent your asking."[13] The psalmist also encourages us to ask: "The eyes of the LORD watch over those who do right; his ears are open to their cries for help."[14] If you keep your hand in the Lord's by reading and studying his Word and crying out for help, he will prompt you to choose wisely.

I have found that the Bible and the Lord are quite faithful to help me know what is right. One day, I went to a large discount department store. Shopping, particularly at this store, is not one of my favorite activities. The carts are huge, the aisles are narrow, the people are plentiful, and the checkout lines are long. But the prices are good, so I go there when necessary.

That morning, I quickly made my way around the store and, to my surprise, found a short line at the checkout. Before I knew it, I was back at my car. As I was unloading my purchases, though, I saw one roll of paper towels on the very bottom of the cart. I looked hard at that roll of paper towels, and the harder I looked, the clearer it became that I had left the store without paying for it. I prayed, *Lord, we're looking at sixty-nine cents here. You know that I'm honest, and I know that I need to pay for this, but I don't want to go back in there and stand in line. It's such a waste of time! Will they ever miss sixty-nine cents? Who will know?* Immediately, in my heart, I heard these words, *Cynthia, a child of mine does what is right. Who will know? I will know. And so will you.*

And so we do what is right because it is right. It is right from God's perspective, and it is right from ours. God wants us to do what is right because it's the very best way for us to live. He doesn't want us to experience the loss, the "if onlys," the guilt that result from doing what is wrong. It often costs us to do what is right, but the rewards are a clear conscience, peace, and joy in knowing that we have followed *in his steps.*

I included Ben in my luncheon and later reluctantly took back the paper towels because my life is God's. I am his child, and I want to do what is right because I love him. I want my actions to bring him glory—even if the Lord and I are the only ones who know of my decision. That, in a way, is the best kind of glory—doing what is right whether or not anyone else knows.

The Lord knows, and that is enough.

*Listen as Wisdom calls out!*
*Hear as understanding raises her voice! . . .*
*Listen to me! For I have important things to tell you.*
*Everything I say is right,*
*for I speak the truth*
*and detest every kind of deception.*

PROVERBS 8:1; 6-7

# A Prayer for Wisdom

Heavenly Father, thank you that I am on the narrow way, the way that leads to life. Give me new eyes to see your way clearly and to see your love and goodness within that way. Give me insight into your Word so that I can discern what is right. Teach me wisdom's ways. Let me be sensitive to your Spirit when he whispers, "This is the way, walk in it."[15] May my desire to be righteous spring out of my passion to be like Christ. I pray with the psalmist: "Oh, that my steps might be steady, keeping to the course you set; Then I'd never have any regrets in comparing my life with your counsel."[16] In Jesus' name, amen.

# Reflections on the Truth

1. In today's world, the lines between what is right and what is wrong tend to blur. What is your greatest struggle in choosing the right response or the right path?

2. It's God's love for you that asks you to do what is right; he is concerned for your welfare. What do the following verses indicate about how the godly are blessed?

   a. Psalm 84:11-12

   b. Psalm 106:3

   c. Proverbs 21:3

3. You need wisdom to do the right thing. Read Proverbs 2:1-11, and write down how you can find wisdom and the blessings that accompany wisdom.

4. The psalmist David asked God for help in doing the right thing. Using Psalm 25:4-5 as a guide, write down your own prayer asking God to show you what is right.

# Scripture to Believe

Give yourselves completely to God since you have been given new life. And use your whole body as a tool to do what is right for the glory of God.

ROMANS 6:13, NLT-1996

EIGHT

# LOVE IS NOT OPTIONAL

*Only love is completely self-sufficient, for only love has nothing whatsoever to lose in spilling itself out, since that is its very nature. Only love is so inwardly strong and deeply confident of itself that it does not ever need to retaliate, even against its bitterest enemies. Love alone stands alone, through having already surrendered everything.*

MIKE MASON, *The Mystery of Marriage*

*[Jesus said,] "So now I am giving you a new commandment: Love each other. Just as I have loved you, you should love each other."*

JOHN 13:34

MY DAD WAS A MAN OF CONTRADICTIONS. One side of him lived to enjoy life, to have fun, and to make things happen. Our family went to all the major sporting events, attended barbershop-quartet conventions as well as circuses and movies. He was an amateur cook, whose specialties were barbecue and buttermilk pancakes. His favorite saying while we were eating was, "Isn't this good? Don't you wish your throat were three feet long?" Whenever he cooked, however, the kitchen was left in shambles. He would leave behind charred kitchen towels and pot holders along with batter and sauce drippings on the countertops and floor. It took a few years before my brother, my mom, and I were able to laugh about the hours we spent cleaning the kitchen, especially after he fried chicken.

Dad loved to go to movies, where after about an hour, he promptly went to sleep. One of my fondest memories is the day he took me to see four movies in a row. I'll never forget him looking down at me and asking with a grin, "Want to go to another one?"

All of this sounds good, but the other side of my dad was not so pleasant. It made him a hard man to love. He was completely self-absorbed and thought everyone wanted to do what he desired. One time, when he wanted our family to play canasta, he got out the cards and said, "Let's play."

My brother responded, "I don't want to play."

"Yes, you do!" my father replied. My brother and I often tease each other with this memorable phrase.

Dad played golf and also spent long hours in the club-house, playing cards and enjoying the bar. Often, he would forget how long he had been there and would come in after dinner or later—with no call or concern about us. To say the least, his pursuit of what he thought was the "good life" continually caused tension in our home.

In his own way, I think, my dad loved me, but he did not express it very well. For most of my childhood, he called me "Butchie." Hardly a lovely, feminine name. The message I received was that I should have been a boy. Yet when my brother was born, for some reason, my father wasn't pleased about that, either. He felt threatened by my brother's abilities and success, and Dad caused him heartache throughout his life.

My dad was prone to angry outbursts, often targeting my mother. My brother and I never knew when a quarrel would disrupt our home. When I was a young girl, I often went to sleep crying because of the harsh arguments between my mom and dad. One of my painful childhood memories was the time I invited a friend to take a road trip with us. My parents had an argument and didn't speak to each other for two days. I was mortified. As a result, I rarely invited friends to our home.

After I was married, I became apprehensive every time I was with my dad. When he visited our home, he took charge of all our activities and meals. He always had to be the center of attention. The good part was that our children loved him because he was full of life and liked to take them everywhere. But I was always apprehensive about what he might say or do.

I believe it was the humor writer Erma Bombeck who once said about herself, "I don't have stress, but I think I'm a carrier."[1] This described my dad: He didn't have stress, but he certainly was a carrier. Over the years, his stressful personality caused permanent scars for my mother, brother, and me. Consequently, it was hard for me to love this unpredictable man.

My tendency was to respond to him the way many people respond to dysfunction: I distanced myself from him and limited the time I spent in his presence. I buried my feelings, tried to ignore the past, and just got on with my life. Love was not an option for me.

The problem with this way of coping is that it is not God's way.

Shortly before Jesus' crucifixion, he taught his disciples some important principles that would guide them after he had died. He gave them a new command: "Love each other. Just as I have loved you, you should love each other."[2] What does it mean to love others as Christ loves us? Christ's love is unconditional, sacrificial, and everlasting. That's a tall order. When I allowed that challenging command to sink into my heart, I realized I was not following it, especially in my relationship with my dad. I loved him when he was lovable. I loved him when it was convenient. But my love certainly wasn't consistent.

Jesus' Sermon on the Mount has been paraphrased in this

way: "I'm telling you to love your enemies. Let them bring out the best in you, not the worst. When someone gives you a hard time, respond with the energies of prayer, for then you are working out of your true selves, your God-created selves."[3] I would not say my father was my enemy, but one definition of an enemy is a "hostile unit."[4] Unpredictable as he was, his behavior often made our home feel a bit like a war zone.

I had embarked on a journey of following Christ, and suddenly the signposts on this narrow road all pointed to my need to love, for Jesus was clear that we must love each other as he has loved us.

These words have penetrated deep into my soul and convicted me. When I feel rejected, mistreated, or wounded, my first response is not to love. I usually withdraw and dwell on my hurt.

I've tried to find some contingency clause in Christ's command to love, something like, "Love one another, but if they treat you unfairly or hurt you or oppose you, well, then you can back off." I wanted some options, perhaps a "kind" retaliation, a limp handshake as I withdrew from a friendship, at least a heavy sigh and shrug of the shoulders—something to show others my hurt and disappointment.

But Jesus' teaching leaves no escape clause. As I studied, I discovered that no matter who has hurt us, no matter what the person has done, even if they are our enemy, *love is not optional*. Love is nonnegotiable.

Jesus said to "Love your enemies! Do good to those who

hate you."[5] The apostle Paul taught: "'If your enemies are hungry, feed them. If they are thirsty, give them something to drink, and they will be ashamed of what they have done to you.' Don't let evil get the best of you, but conquer evil by doing good."[6]

Doing good to our enemies involves being sensitive to their needs and creatively seeking to serve them in love. Holly told me about her irritable neighbor who seemed to complain about everything: noisy children, basketballs in the yard, or too many cars parked in the street. Her family had to be careful about anything that might provoke their neighbor. Holly knew the Scripture verse about doing good to those who hate you. As she prayed about how to relate to her neighbor, she was amazed at what the Lord prompted her to do: pull the weeds in her "enemy's" yard. As Holly worked in her neighbor's front yard, she could sense her neighbor watching from inside the house. This woman never acknowledged Holly's work, but eventually the complaining began to subside. Holly conquered evil by doing good.

My close friend Diane also learned to love someone who was difficult: her mother-in-law, whom she referred to as her "thorn in the flesh." Here are my friend's own words:

[My mother-in-law] came to live with us at the age of seventy-nine. . . . We had been married for nine years and had four small children. "Mom" was determined to get as much attention as possible from my busy doctor husband, who was rarely home. She

would rise early—four or five in the morning—
and start banging a spoon on the kitchen table,
announcing that it was time for her coffee.

She insisted on never being alone, which
meant I couldn't even go to the bathroom alone.
"*Diaaane*," followed by knocks on the door, could
be heard throughout the house. Car pools were not
immune to her, either. She became a fixture in the
front passenger seat—with her hand on the horn
if I walked a child inside and took too long. She
was also a *joy* to shop with. When buying school
clothes, I would find a comfy chair for her in the
shoe department before heading out. Ten minutes
later, I would inevitably hear my name paged over
the loudspeaker system![7]

Diane tried to love her mother-in-law, but nothing my
friend did ever pleased her. On the outside, Diane went
through the motions, but inside, she was resentful.

One night, after Diane had been awakened by a phone
call, she could not go back to sleep, so she decided to spend
time with the Lord and his Word. She read the Crucifixion
story, where Jesus commits his mother, Mary, to the care of
the disciple John. Diane writes,

With great tenderness and compassion, [Christ]
says to John, "Here is your mother." Tears filled my
eyes and my heart burned as my Lord said to *me*,

"Here is your mother." . . . Was I not also a disciple?
Was I not also commanded to love others as He had
loved me?

My heart changed that night. God gave me His
heart for Mom.[8]

And exactly what is God's heart toward us? No one por-
trays the depth and persistence of God's heart for us like the
Old Testament prophet Hosea, who lived during the eighth
century BC and prophesied to the ten northern tribes known
as Israel. God called Hosea to give a graphic and dramatic
message of his love in an unusual and unforgettable way.

God directed Hosea to marry a prostitute as an object
lesson to Israel of the Lord's love and faithfulness to his sinful children: "Go and marry a prostitute, so that some of her
children will be conceived in prostitution. This will illustrate
how Israel has acted like a prostitute by turning against the
LORD and worshiping other gods."[9]

Hosea obeyed the Lord and married Gomer, who,
after experiencing Hosea's love and comfort, ran away and
became the slave or concubine of another man. To portray
his unconditional love and grace, God asked Hosea to go and
buy Gomer back—to redeem her. The Bible tells us: "The
LORD still loves Israel, even though the people have turned
to other gods and love to worship them."[10]

Although God's beloved, the people of Israel, turned away
from him just as Gomer turned away from Hosea, the Lord
wanted his beloved to know that no matter what they did,

he loved them and was committed to them as their true husband. The overpowering message of the book of Hosea is that love is everlasting and not optional.

But this is indeed a difficult truth to put into practice. How can we love when what we really want to do is to repay someone who has hurt us? How can we extend love when everything in us wants to receive love, wants to be protected, wants to do what feels right to us? How can we love when we feel so inadequate to love as God loves us? I struggle with these questions frequently, and I have to continually remind myself to readjust the cross on my shoulder so that when my "self" tries to exercise control and interfere with my loving someone who has hurt me, I have the freedom to choose love over self.

I can begin to love only when I recognize that God doesn't expect me to love with my own strength. He knows that I'm incapable of loving as he loves. I can begin to love only when I realize that it's God's love within me, through his Holy Spirit, that is able to love others through me. "We know how dearly God loves us, because he has given us the Holy Spirit to fill our hearts with his love."[11]

When we invite Christ into our lives, he plants his love in our hearts. As we abide in his love, he equips us to walk in his Spirit and receive the power and love that come from keeping our hands in his. The Lord has not asked us to do something that is impossible; what he does ask is that we understand that love is not optional.

Why is love not optional? I had always thought that God commands us to love because other people need us to love them. What I have discovered, though, is that when we love, *we* are the ones who benefit. The antithesis of love is hate. If we live with anger and hate, *we* are the ones who experience the destruction and debilitation. When Christ tells us to love and forgive others, he is thinking about our welfare. Love heals, blesses, and frees *us*. His command for us to love others is a reflection of his great love for us. The Scriptures remind us,

God showed how much he loved us by sending his one and only Son into the world so that we might have eternal life through him. This is real love—not that we loved God, but that he loved us and sent his Son as a sacrifice to take away our sins.

Dear friends, since God loved us that much, we surely ought to love each other.[12]

I remember that point in my life when I understood that I was not only to honor my dad but also to express love for him as Christ has done for me. I knew that my father needed to sense my acceptance instead of my frustration. I wanted him to experience the love of Christ, if only through me. It was extremely difficult, but my first step in loving my dad was to release him to the Lord. I did that by praying, "Lord, I give you my father. Help me to accept him just the way he is. I know that I cannot change him, but I want to do what is right and give him your love. Teach me to love my dad so that he will be drawn to you."

The result of that prayer was a gradual, growing love for who my dad was. I was able to see him through different eyes, through God's eyes. I was startled to realize that I could think of no one who really loved my dad. This man was desperate for love. When my dad became ill, he also became afraid. God gave my brother and me time to share with him about the good news of Christ. Dad listened, and we were able to read Scripture passages with him and pray with him.

I did not see a drastic change in my dad, but I do feel that he met the Lord. He began to read some of the Bible, and in his last months, he told me what a good nurse my mother was. I think he finally came to appreciate her gifts. Choosing to love my dad is one decision I have never regretted, for it was the right thing to do. Again, I learned in an incredible, precious way that maybe God is right after all.

Diane knew that God was right when he asked her to love her mother-in-law as he loved her. Here is the rest of her story:

No longer was it an effort to love and care for her. She lived with us for sixteen years, and we now see her time with us as a divine gift to bring supernatural love into our family. It was the Lord who asked for a gentle and quiet spirit from me—and it was this thorn of adversity that caused me to learn how to walk in the Spirit and not in the flesh. I fell more and more in love with Jesus—and my husband—as I practiced on "His mom."[13]

When I was a new Christian, someone told me that within fifteen minutes of meeting someone, the other person should be able to discern "something" different about me. I think this "something" should be the love of Christ dwelling within me; Christ's love should be growing to the extent that people can see it reflected in my life. God is faithful as he gently and consistently conforms me to the image of his Son by showing me, time and again, when I am unloving.

I love that God's command is so clear-cut, understandable, and wise. If I want to obey, then I will choose to love. It is by necessity then, that if I am to do what he asks, I must keep my hand in his day by day and allow him to change my life by continually teaching me to live wisely by understanding that love is not optional.

*Imitate God, therefore, in everything you do, because you are his dear children. Live a life filled with love, following the example of Christ. He loved us and offered himself as a sacrifice for us, a pleasing aroma to God.*

EPHESIANS 5:1-2

## A Prayer for Wisdom

Heavenly Father, I know that your command to love blesses others and is for my good. I am most grateful for your

Holy Spirit, who fills my heart with your love. Enable me to empty myself, to surrender everything, so that I might know this love that extends grace and mercy.

Continue to teach and mold me so that my love will be a natural response to others. May I grow in patience and kindness. Keep me from being proud, rude, and irritable, and keep me from dwelling on when I have been wronged. Help me to understand that love has nothing to lose in spilling itself out. May I love others just as you love me. I ask in Christ's name, amen.

## Reflections on the Truth

1.  I shared about how hard it was to love my dad. Who is the "thorn in the flesh" in your life, the person whom you struggle to love? In what way are you encouraged to love that person or others now?

2.  Read the following verses, and write down how you think God sees this person. Substitute his or her name in the verses, if possible, as in the example.

    a.  John 3:16, NLT-2007—"God loved [name] so much that he gave his one and only Son, so that everyone [name] who believes in him will not perish but have eternal life."

    b.  Romans 5:6-8

3. After meditating on Romans 5:5, write a prayer asking God to fill you and give you his love to extend to this difficult person.

## Scripture to Believe

[Jesus said,] "Now I am giving you a new commandment: Love each other. Just as I have loved you, you should love each other."

JOHN 13:34

# NINE

# FORGIVENESS FREES
# THE FORGIVER

*I do not believe that my family deserves forgiveness, but that is not the point. I longed to be free from the bitterness and rage that were destroying me. Slowly, I began to open myself up to the possibility of forgiveness, and my life began to change. God softened my heart and filled me with love. It was like opening the windows on a beautiful spring day. I believe that forgiveness is part of the healing process and is itself a process. Forgiveness has little to do with your abuser. Forgiveness is about freedom from destructive thoughts and emotions. Forgiveness is about fellowship with God.*

A SURVIVOR OF SEXUAL ABUSE, quoted in
Diane Mandt Langberg, *On the Threshold of Hope*

*[Jesus said,] "When you are praying, first forgive anyone you are holding a grudge against, so that your Father in heaven will forgive your sins, too."*

MARK 11:25

CORRIE TEN BOOM WAS NOT surprised that February morning in 1944 when the gestapo burst into her family's home and started smashing cupboards and doors. For months, she and her family had been hiding Jews in a secret room above her father's watch shop in Haarlem, the Netherlands, hoping to save them from being sent to German concentration camps. Corrie had known it was only a matter of time before their underground activities were discovered. That day, Corrie and her family were arrested and placed in a Dutch prison. Corrie never saw her father again; he died in his prison cell ten days later.

After months of being shifted from one prison to another, Corrie and her sister, Betsie, were carted off to the Ravensbrück concentration camp, where they suffered harsh treatment and extreme deprivation at the hands of the Nazi guards. Corrie called it "the deepest hell that man can create."[1]

Betsie became very ill, seriously weakening day after day. Corrie took her to the camp infirmary, begging the nurses to help her sister. But Betsie languished and died. A short time later, Corrie was released; she learned afterward that her discharge had been the result of a mistake, a clerical error. A week after she left, all the women of her age in the camp were killed.[2]

Ten years later, Corrie met a woman whom she discovered had been a nurse at the concentration camp. Corrie remembered the nurse's cruelty when she had taken Betsie to the infirmary. The memories rekindled Corrie's resentment, and her rage almost overcame her. Desperately, she prayed, "Forgive me." She cried out to the Lord, "Forgive my hatred, O Lord. Teach me to love my enemies."

After praying, Corrie felt her rage replaced with a divine love that she couldn't explain. She began praying for the nurse and eventually called her at the hospital and invited her to attend a speaking engagement. The nurse was touched that Corrie had called her, and after the meeting, Corrie was able to introduce the nurse to the Lord Jesus.[3]

As I contemplated how Corrie must have felt after speaking with the nurse, I thought that she probably felt a deep joy and a wonderful sense of freedom. Reflecting on how she might have felt if she had not forgiven the nurse, I knew that the anger and bitterness would have invaded her heart and settled in to stay. Although she was no longer physically in prison, she would have entered an emotional prison of her own choosing.

Corrie wisely understood that she had to deal with her anger and rage, and she immediately prayed for God to help her love her enemy. She knew if she didn't forgive, she would be shut in by the iron bars of resentment instead of experiencing the open window of forgiveness.

This is upside-down thinking. Our natural instincts are to make the other person suffer as we have suffered. Our normal response to people who hurt us is revenge. We cling to our rights, protect ourselves, nurse our grudges so that we can in some way repay the perpetrators. Something in us says that releasing the offender is wrong. We think that if we forgive someone who has wounded us, that person will never be held accountable.

Jesus knew this about the human heart, so he clearly told his followers what he expected from them. I can only imagine what the crowds must have thought when they heard him proclaim, "Do good to those who hate you. . . . Pray for those who hurt you. . . . Forgive others, and you will be forgiven."[4] Who was this man with such radical teaching? Why should we do good things to those we hate? It doesn't make sense to pray for those who hurt us. Why is God's forgiveness of me dependent on my forgiving others?

Christ's teaching is just as extraordinary today as it was two thousand years ago. These commands seem to destroy any sense of "self" and any rights I might have. What happens to *me* if I forgive? What happens to my offender?

My young friend Amy came to my home to share with me a deep hurt that she had been struggling with for years. The burden she carried had come from her father's abuse. She had read several books, sought good counsel, and when she came to talk with me, I think she was finally ready to accept Jesus' teaching about forgiveness.

Her questions were normal. She said, "It doesn't seem fair for me to let my father off the hook. He should be made to suffer for what he did to me. Everyone thinks he is such a good Christian man—if only they knew what he is really like."

I listened and agreed with her that to respond by releasing

and forgiving her father seemed to go against our sense of how to right a wrong. Although I could not begin to identify with her pain, I could understand her struggle over freeing herself from her father. I shared my experience of clearly hearing the Lord's prompting to release my dad, to accept him as he was, and to forgive him. I told Amy that forgiving my father was the best decision not only for me but also for him.

Amy and I read together a verse in Romans: "Dear friends, never take revenge. Leave that to the righteous anger of God. For the Scriptures say, '*I* will take revenge; *I* will pay them back,' says the LORD."[5]

I explained to her, "God wants to free us from ever having to vindicate ourselves. Vengeance is God's responsibility. So, you are not really letting your father off the hook; you are just releasing him to the only one who is just, fair, and able to correct or repay those who harm us.

"One of the most precious lessons I've learned from God is that he asks me to forgive because he loves me and wants me to be free—free from bitterness and free to love even when it is hard. Forgiving and releasing my dad blessed me and my dad. I have never regretted my decision to forgive him. Especially now, since he died, I'm so thankful that we had a few years in which I was free to relate to him in a way that pleased God."

Amy was understandably hesitant about going to her father. I said, "Amy, the most important thing is that you forgive your dad. This forgiveness is between you and God. Forgiveness is essentially vertical; reconciliation is horizontal.

After the vertical is taken care of, then trust God to guide in how to be reconciled. Pray and ask the Lord about if—or when and where—you need to talk with your dad. Surrender your situation to God, and let him guide you in the right way to relate to your dad. Sometimes sharing with the other person is needed, but it is not always necessary or beneficial."

It was not easy for Amy to forgive her dad. It is never *easy*, but it is right—for us. We are the ones who benefit.

It also was not easy for Betty Ferguson to forgive the English teacher who abducted and murdered her sixteen-year-old daughter. Betty was consumed by hatred. She neglected her other children and suffered from severe headaches and back pain. This went on for six years, until she attended a funeral and heard Jesus' words from the Lord's Prayer: "Forgive us our sins, as we have forgiven those who sin against us."[6]

For the first time, Betty's heart opened to the possibility of forgiving the murderer. She wrote to him and eventually went to visit him in prison. He listened to her feelings of devastation. They both cried, and when Betty left, she was a different person. She said, "My heart felt soft and light and warm." When her friends questioned what she had done, she answered, "Forgiveness is the greatest gift I ever gave myself—and my children."[7]

God is so clear about our forgiving others because he wants us to experience the gift of forgiveness. Forgiveness frees the forgiver from debilitating emotions that undermine and deplete our emotional and physical reserves. King Solomon reminds us: "A calm and undisturbed mind and heart are the life and health of the body, but envy, jealousy, and wrath are like rottenness of the bones."[8] The apostle Paul expresses similar truth in his letter to the Ephesian believers: "Get rid of all bitterness, rage, anger, harsh words, and slander, as well as all types of evil behavior. Instead, be kind to each other, tenderhearted, forgiving one another, just as God through Christ has forgiven you."[9]

Not only do harmful emotions damage us emotionally, but, as the Scriptures teach, these runaway emotions also corrode our bones. The abuse survivor quoted at the beginning of this chapter said that she longed to be free from the bitterness and rage that were destroying her. God wants us to forgive because he knows that a freed heart will lead to emotional and physical health.

I have been amazed at how important our forgiving others is to God. Jesus not only taught us to pray "Forgive us our sins, as we have forgiven those who sin against us,"[10] but he also reinforced this vital lesson by adding a powerful and stunning PS: "If you forgive those who sin against you, your heavenly Father will forgive you. But if you refuse to forgive others, your Father will not forgive your sins."[11] He could not have been more clear about how significant forgiveness is to our own spiritual well-being.

It's not that God doesn't want to forgive us; it's that a revengeful spirit keeps God at a distance. Pride drives us to hold on to our "right" to retaliate, to hold on to the hurt. We become our own god and therefore have no need for the living and true God.

How tragic that we set ourselves up for continual heart-ache and suffering, even though the Lord has so wonderfully promised to look after us. Liz's parents had a bitter divorce, and each one told her that if she visited the other parent, then she was no longer welcome. This exemplifies how blinding revenge can be: "I'll punish the one who hurt me by not seeing my daughter." It also exemplifies how unforgiveness affects all those who are close to us. Liz and her family were caught between her parents' bitterness toward each other; my friend was forced to choose sides.

In learning to forgive, we must understand how to handle our feelings. There can be times when we earnestly pray to forgive someone yet we find that the feelings don't go away and resentment keeps surfacing. We question whether we have really forgiven and begin to think that forgiveness really doesn't work. This is when we need to remember that forgiveness is often a process.

Paula Rinehart observes,

Some injuries of the spirit have both a past and an ongoing present—and so forgiveness by necessity is a work in progress. A woman whose husband has been addicted to pornography forgives—but she may well be faced with the problem again. When she climbs into bed with her husband, you can be sure that she is making an ongoing choice to forgive and to rebuild trust. . . .

. . . Forgiving well means moving through the hurt and the legitimate anger that tells us we've been hurt, to a choice to release the person who inflicted the injury. . . . Forgiveness is about looking the pain straight in the eye and saying, "God is bigger than this."[12]

Remember Brian Birdwell, who was severely burned when the terrorists crashed a plane into the Pentagon on September 11, 2001? He is quite honest about his journey of forgiveness:

When I look where I've been and where I am now, God is absolutely gracious. So if I were bitter now, after having come through the last three years, that bitterness would be grossly displaced.

Do I desire to see justice served? Absolutely! But do I sit and stew or bemoan my altered life? No. We serve a magnificent God. As a Christian I work through the process of forgiving those who hurt me because I know ultimately God will judge rightly and the people who chose evil will receive their just reward. . . .

And yet it's going to take a long time to forgive and move on. This is probably the toughest part of my faith. I'm learning how to forgive when forgiveness doesn't come easily. I think it will take years for me to completely forgive.[13]

I think that God is pleased when we are honest about how hard it is for us to forgive. The key is our willingness to be in the process of learning how to forgive.

Job, the wealthy Old Testament businessman who lost everything, certainly had to deal with forgiving his friends who falsely accused him and did not speak truthfully about God. It is interesting to me that God instructs Job's friends to offer a sacrifice for their misrepresentation of who he really is. He tells these men: "My servant Job will pray for you, and I will accept his prayer on your behalf."[14] What is remarkable is what happens when Job prays. The Scriptures state: "When Job prayed for his friends, the LORD restored his fortunes."[15] As I have meditated on this verse, I feel that Job's prayer for these men not only interceded on their behalf but also released Job from any ongoing bitterness toward them. God wanted Job to pray, and as he prayed, the Lord was able to bless him. Commentator W. F. Adeney writes concerning Job: "He could afford to forgive when he had himself been graciously accepted by God. The best vengeance we can have on those who ill-treat us is to pray for them, not in hypocritical self-righteousness, but in true-hearted, unaffected kindness. This is Christ's method. He subdues his enemies by dying for them."[16] Forgiveness frees the forgiver, and our forgiving spirit allows God to work in our lives for good.

Nancy Guthrie grappled with forgiving the friends who had not been as supportive as she and her husband expected as they moved through their deep trials of losing two children. She also was interested in Job's prayer. She comments:

I find it somewhat curious that God's instructions to Job were to pray for his friends, until I realize how difficult it is for me to be unforgiving toward someone I am praying for. I wonder if that is why God gave Job those instructions.

If you and I want to be free of the bitterness that estranges us from others and eats away at our own struggle to find joy again, we are going to have to forgive and pray for the friends who have let us down. They might not deserve it. In fact, they probably don't. But then, we don't forgive people because they deserve it; we forgive them because we've been forgiven so much by God and because we want to keep in close relationship with God. And the benefit is that through forgiving, we're set free.[17]

Nancy reminds us that we forgive because we have been forgiven. In the Lord's Prayer, Jesus seems to teach—all in one breath—that we are to ask not only for forgiveness but also for a forgiving spirit: "Forgive us our sins, as we have forgiven those who sin against us."[18] God's forgiveness of us and our forgiveness of others are inescapably bound together.

Whenever I read the New Testament story of the Pharisees brashly taking the woman they caught in adultery to Jesus to be condemned, I put myself in her position. There she was, a pawn in the hands of the Pharisees, used only to trap Jesus. Her life was nothing to them, and she realized that she was about to be stoned to death. Brought before Jesus, her heart racing, she heard the men ask him: "Teacher . . . this woman was caught in the very act of adultery. The law of Moses says to stone her. What do you say?"[19] Jesus answered, "All right, stone her. But let those who have never sinned throw the first stones!"[20]

Her heart must have stopped, and I'm sure that she could barely breathe. She was going to die a cruel death. She waited for the Pharisees to take her away, but one by one they left, and she stood alone. Jesus tenderly and graciously told her that since her accusers didn't condemn her, neither did he. He sent her away with blessed words: "Go and sin no more."[21]

This woman immediately experienced the incredible freedom that being forgiven brings. She was guilty but set free to begin a new life. As I've thought about her, I've wondered how she felt about the Pharisees. Was she filled with anger and resentment? Did she want revenge? Did she talk about how hateful they were?

I don't think she did. Because of the Pharisees' accusations, she met Jesus, who redeemed her, forgave her, and restored her. I believe that she echoed the words Joseph said to his brothers after they had betrayed him: "As far as I am concerned, God turned into good what you meant for evil."[22] I believe the adulterous woman was free to forgive the Pharisees because she realized God was much greater than their evil, and because she had been forgiven, she could forgive.

The good news is that no matter what we have done or what has been done to us, we can experience the extravagant love and forgiveness of God, and we have the honor of extending that forgiveness to others. It is a freeing, blessed, and wise way to live.

> *LORD, if you kept a record of our sins,*
> *who, O Lord, could ever survive?*
> *But you offer forgiveness,*
> *that we might learn to fear you.*

PSALM 130:3-4

# A Prayer for Wisdom

Heavenly Father, how undeserving I am of your enduring love, grace, and forgiveness. It is so easy for me to dwell on the unkindness and hurt that I experience from others. I pray that I will remember that since you bestow forgiveness, I should also. Holding on to resentment is not your way. It is not wise. I confess that it doesn't seem right to forgive, but it is right to obey what you have asked me to do, and that is to release those who have wounded me. Thank you that with forgiveness comes your precious gift of freedom. In Jesus' name, amen.

# Reflections on the Truth

1. When we accept God's sacrificial love and forgiveness, we are privileged to become his children. As you read the following passages, write down how God makes this fellowship possible.

   a. Psalm 86:5-7

   b. Micah 7:18-20

   c. Ephesians 1:6-8

2. If you are struggling with forgiving someone, meditate on Colossians 3:12. Compose a prayer asking the Lord to give you his strength and help in making allowance for another's faults by forgiving and releasing the one who has offended you.

# Scripture to Believe

[Jesus said,] "When you are praying, first forgive anyone you are holding a grudge against, so that your Father in heaven will forgive your sins, too."

MARK 11:25

# TEN

# IT'S GOD'S LIFE

*It does require the supernatural grace of God to live twenty-four hours in every day as a saint, to go through drudgery as a disciple, to live an ordinary, unobserved, ignored existence as a disciple of Jesus. It is inbred in us that we have to do exceptional things for God; but we have not. We have to be exceptional in the ordinary things.*

OSWALD CHAMBERS, *My Utmost for His Highest*

*What can I offer the LORD*
    *for all he has done for me?*
PSALM 116:12

WHILE LIVING IN THE OLD DUPLEX and taking care of three small children, I felt like I was living an ordinary, unobserved, ignored existence as a disciple of Jesus. As I went about my daily regimen, I often thought, *I have a college degree. I am capable of communicating intellectually to rational adults and even making some kind of contribution to society. But here I am in a repetitive routine of reading the ABCs, bathing, feeding, dressing, and then getting up the next day and starting all over again.* I remember praying, "Lord, I feel tied down with the everydayness of life. Am I supposed to just endure this season in my life and wait to make some contribution to your Kingdom or society sometime in the future?"

I felt this way because our lives are often judged and defined by how we spend our days. How often are we asked, "What do you do?"

Not only do others judge and place a value on what we do and what position we hold but we also judge ourselves. It's easy to get discouraged when we feel trapped by our circumstances. Situations that limit our ability to live or serve in the way we think we should can close in on us and make us feel as if we are wasting time.

Having three children was a special blessing from God, and it was wrong for me to feel confined and useless. I was thinking only of myself and choosing to be ungrateful and discontent. I was not willing to live exceptionally in the ordinary.

Although my feelings were real, my daily life paled in

comparison to so many others. Countless people endure overwhelming circumstances and confront feelings of hopelessness because they see no purpose for their lives. As Gracia Burnham endured her captivity at the hands of terrorists in the Philippines, she became depressed and angry at God. She felt that God did not love her because he was not coming through for her and her husband, Martin. One day, Gracia realized that she had a choice in how she could respond to her circumstances. She writes:

> I could give in to my resentment and allow it to dig me into a deeper and deeper hole both psychologically and emotionally, or I could choose to believe what God's Word says to be true whether I felt it was or not.
>
> This was a turning point for me. It was as if God were saying to me, "If you're going to believe that I died for you, why not believe that I love you?" . . .
>
> . . . More than once, Martin said to me, "Maybe God has us here just to praise him in this very dark place."
>
> Gradually, my crisis of faith passed. I realized it would do no good to be angry with God. He had neither inspired the Abu Sayyaf to abduct us nor would he force them against their will to release us. Instead, he would sustain us day by day, night by night, mile by mile, for as long as it took.[1]

Very few of us will ever experience what Gracia did, but many of us will have to face our own dark places and wonder how God could receive glory. My friend Janell, who cares for her eighty-five-year-old mother, has just been given custody of her five-year-old grandson. Lucy, a working single mom, is raising four children. Angie is caring for both of her elderly parents. Helen is struggling with MS. Doris is nursing her husband as she watches him slowly succumb to cancer. I know that each one of these women is trusting God to sustain her "day by day, night by night" as she is embraced by his love. These women, despite their circumstances, are living for his glory.

These are all hard places to be, but our hope and our purpose are found in the unshakable truths that God is for us, that he can be trusted especially when life doesn't make sense, that we will never regret doing what is right, and that our lives are God's—to be lived for his glory, no matter how painful or ordinary our circumstances might be.

Scripture records the stories of many individuals who lived exceptional lives in commonplace circumstances. They accepted their seemingly insignificant and trying situations as opportunities to serve to the glory of God.

I have always been challenged by the unswerving commitment of the armor bearer who served Jonathan, the son of King Saul in the Old Testament. The armor bearer's job was to carry Jonathan's weapons, stand by him in danger, and deliver his orders to others. On one occasion, Jonathan decided to take his armor bearer and see if they could do battle with the Philistine army on their own: "Let's go across to see those pagans," Jonathan said to his aide. "Perhaps the LORD will help us, for nothing can hinder the LORD. He can win a battle whether he has many warriors or only a few!" The armor bearer replied, "Do what you think is best. . . . I'm with you completely, whatever you decide."[2] This unnamed aide was willing to risk his life to fulfill his duty. He was only an armor bearer, but he fulfilled his role wholeheartedly.

I've also often thought of the young Israelite slave who served the wife of Naaman, an Old Testament Syrian army commander who had leprosy. The Scriptures tell us, "One day the girl said to her mistress, 'I wish my master would go to see the prophet in Samaria. He would heal him of his leprosy.'"[3] What impresses me about this young woman is that she was truly concerned about this man, who captured her, took her away from her family, and made her a slave. Although her life was no longer her own and she served in humble, routine ways, she was willing to share her faith and care for her master's welfare. She was exceptional in the ordinary.

The Old Testament prophet Amos was a plain Judean shepherd who also tended fig trees. Out of these ordinary circumstances, God called him to announce judgment, primarily on the people of Israel. In Bethel, Amos encountered the priest Amaziah, who threatened the prophet and charged him with conspiracy against the king. When Amaziah ordered Amos out of Bethel, the prophet replied, "I'm not one of your professional prophets. I certainly never trained to be one. I'm just a shepherd, and I take care of fig trees. But the LORD called me away from my flock and told me, 'Go and prophesy to my people in Israel.'"[4] Amos was only a normal, run-of-the-mill shepherd, but his life belonged to God, and he was willing to do whatever God asked of him.

In the community of Joppa, Dorcas (also called Tabitha) was known for her kindness and mercy. The New Testament describes her life this way: "She was always doing kind things for others and helping the poor."[5] When she became ill and died, her death deeply affected the church and the poor people of Joppa. When the apostle Peter arrived at Dorcas's home, he found the room filled with mourners, who were weeping and showing him garments she had made for them. Peter performed a great miracle by restoring this godly woman to life. Why was Dorcas so greatly loved? She was a gifted seamstress whose life belonged to God, and she gave him glory by serving others in his name.

The armor bearer, the servant girl, Amos, and Dorcas all were willing to live God's life where they were. They were living sacrifices who made their ordinary lives available for God to use.[6]

Oswald Chambers describes the apostle Paul as a person who "attracted [people] to Jesus all the time, never to himself. . . . Paul became a sacramental personality; wherever he [Paul] went, Jesus Christ helped Himself to his life."[7] I am so struck by this description, and I have made it my prayer that God will help himself to my life wherever I am so that I might bring him glory and bear fruit. Jesus said, "My true disciples produce much fruit. This brings great glory to my Father."[8] When we live God's life, we bear the fruit of Christlike character and are conscious of being his ambassadors so that others will be attracted to Jesus. We go about our day-to-day lives sensitive to his Spirit and ready to honor and represent him in whatever we do.

I met Carrie at a conference. Although she was a busy mom of three small children, she took advantage of every opportunity to represent Christ in the world. She told me that each time she goes grocery shopping, she purposely chooses to take her groceries to the same checkout clerk. Her goal is to develop a relationship with this woman in order to share the good news of knowing Christ. Carrie's life is God's, even in the grocery store.

God wants us to live wholeheartedly for him, no matter what we do or where we live: "Whatever you eat or drink or whatever you do, you must do all for the glory of God."[9] This simple, uncomplicated instruction is a scriptural truth for all seasons. At the heart of this teaching is the fact that *all* of our daily activities are to be lived for God's glory— because our lives are his. No matter what my situation is at any point in my life, I can say that it's God's life to be lived for his glory.

Isn't it interesting that the apostle Paul mentions eating and drinking in the context of bringing glory to God? If someone asked us what activities would glorify God, we would probably mention preaching or serving or teaching the Bible, not eating and drinking. In his classic devotional book *The Pursuit of God*, A. W. Tozer clarifies: "It is not what a man does that determines whether his work is sacred or secular, it is why he does it. The motive is everything. Let a man sanctify the Lord God in his heart and he can thereafter do no common act. All he does is good and acceptable to God through Jesus Christ."[10]

If we are seeking to honor the Lord, then any activity, no matter how humble or ordinary, takes on spiritual significance. Consequently, our everyday lives have great value and worth. We serve not for earthly applause or self-satisfaction but for the higher and nobler purpose of God's glory.

It took several years for me to learn that though I felt I was not doing anything monumental for the Lord while taking care of our children, what I was doing was exactly what God wanted me to be doing. In *The Life You've Always Wanted*, John Ortberg tells about a young mother with similar feelings:

> A mother in our small group suggested that it was easier for her to "work on her spiritual life" before she became a mom. As we talked, it became clear what she meant. To her, reading the Bible and praying were the only two activities that counted spiritually. . . .
>
> . . . She had never been taught to see that caring for two young children, offered daily with expressions of gratitude and prayers for help and patient acceptance of trials, might become a

kind of school for transformation into powerful servanthood beyond anything she had ever known. Somehow having a "quiet time" *counted* toward spiritual devotion, and caring for two children did not. . . .

*Life counts—all of it.* Every moment is potentially an opportunity to be guided by God into his way of living. Every moment is a chance to learn from Jesus how to live in the kingdom of God.[11]

Now, several decades later, I see how God was guiding me into his way of living. I realize that probably the only way I could ever begin to develop any fruit of the Spirit was to have three children in three years! For twenty-seven years, I served my family; I stayed at my "post." I look back and am amazed that the life God had for me was the perfect preparation for the ministry of becoming an older woman in the body of Christ.

We can live God's life simply by giving a cup of cold water in his name, by walking side by side with others to help carry their load, by cooking, cleaning, sewing, or caring for those who are helpless. Grocery shopping can become a mission field, and choosing to bring God glory can become a lifelong adventure.

"It does require the supernatural grace of God to live twenty-four hours in every day as a saint," Oswald Chambers points out, but the very good news is that we do have God's divine grace, most beautifully communicated through Christ's sacrifice on the cross. That grace is given freely, so we can be free from the tyranny of sin and self. His grace takes us by the hand and leads us in right and true paths. His gracious Word teaches, corrects, and guides us. By his grace, we are free to reject self-centered living and choose a life of love, offering our bodies as living sacrifices to be used for his glory. All of these ideas are true and make it possible to live wisely.

I pray that in whatever circumstance you find yourself (single, single with children, married, married without children, working at a job, or working at home), you will draw on God's supernatural grace to live your life—God's life—for his glory.

How thankful I am that my search for wisdom led me to enter by the narrow gate and that I was able to discover God's revolutionary truth. It has certainly made all the difference. Because God is for me, the heartaches and difficulties I've experienced have been tenderly woven into the fabric of my life for my good. I have had precious moments of sensing the Lord's presence and love for me. My greatest blessings have come from the few times I have chosen to lay myself aside and in some feeble way bring him glory. I am continually in his debt that he gave his life for me and that he graciously adopted me as his child to live with him forever. Truly the best is yet to come.

God is the almighty God—holy, faithful, gracious, loving, and righteous. What can I offer the Lord for all he has done for me? My life—to be lived wisely, wherever I am, for his glory.

*O my God, you are always with me. Since I must now, in obedience to your will for me, apply my mind to my day's work, grant me the grace I shall need to continue through it in your presence. Help me to do this work to your glory. Receive it as a spiritual offering. And let my desire be only to please you.*

THE DAILY PRAYER OF BROTHER LAWRENCE AS HE BEGAN HIS DAY SERVING IN THE KITCHEN OF A MONASTERY, quoted in David Winter, *Closer than a Brother*

# A Prayer for Wisdom

Heavenly Father, words cannot begin to express my deep feelings of love, joy, and gratitude when I realize all you have done for me. As the psalmist sang, "Let all that I am praise the LORD; with my whole heart, I will praise his holy name. Let all that I am praise the LORD; may I never forget the good things he does for me."[12] Lord, do not let me forget the good things you do for me. I know that my life is a gift from you, and I gladly place it back in your hands. Help yourself to my life, Lord, so that by your grace, I might live every day and every situation for your honor and praise. May I sanctify you in my heart so that all I do will bring you glory. In humble adoration, I ask all these things in Jesus' name, amen.

# Reflections on the Truth

1.  In his book *The Pursuit of God*, A. W. Tozer made this observation: "The whole universe is alive with His life."[13] The following verses portray God's relationship with all of creation. How do these passages encourage you to trust God with your life?

    a. Genesis 1:1

    b. Colossians 1:15-18

    c. Revelation 4:11

2.  This book has led us through ten truths of Scripture that help us to live God's life wisely. Think back over what you have read, and respond to the following questions:

    a. Which truth has the potential of making a permanent change in your life?

    b. Why did you choose this truth?

    c. How can this truth transform your life?

3.  Every one of the truths in this book is a practical guideline for living wisely. In your own words, as either a

prayer or a personal reflection, summarize how you want to give your life to God and live it for his glory.

Here is mine:

*It's your life now*
*You formed me, redeemed me;*
*in humbleness I bow.*

*Show me your way.*
*Lead me and teach me;*
*mold me as clay.*

*My future is glory.*
*So with passion I live*
*to finish my story.*

# Scripture to Believe

What can I offer the LORD
for all he has done for me?

PSALM 116:12

A FINAL WORD:

# THE BEST IS YET TO COME

*You will not be in heaven two seconds before you cry out,* "Why did I place so much importance on things that were so temporary? *What was I thinking? Why did I waste so much time, energy, and concern on what wasn't going to last?" When life gets tough, when you're overwhelmed with doubt, or when you wonder if living for Christ is worth the effort, remember that you are not home yet. At death you won't leave home—you'll go home.*

RICK WARREN, *The Purpose-Driven Life*

*What we suffer now is nothing compared to the glory he will give us later.*

ROMANS 8:18, TLB

I HAD JUST RETURNED HOME from attending a memorial service. Our friend Don entered his eternal home at age eighty-one. It was a blessing to hear others speak of his great love for the Lord and for people. It was also a blessing to hear various people reflect on the wonderful experience Don must be having in heaven: "I know Don is rejoicing right now with the God he loved." "Don must be in awe of the beauty and splendor of heaven." "I'm sure Don quickly found the place that the Lord had prepared for him."

As I left the memorial service, I found myself a little envious of Don. He is in the presence of the Lord. He has seen Jesus face-to-face. He is whole and will never again experience weariness, fear, or hurt. For Don, the best has come. He is finally home.

I was envious because when I experience difficulty and just want to run away from it all, I find myself praying as the psalmist David prayed, "Oh, how I wish I had wings like a dove; then I would fly away and rest!"[1] Essentially, I am saying, "I want out of here! I want to go someplace where I don't have to struggle with loving those who are hard to love, where I will no longer experience emotional pain, where I don't have to deal with my sinful nature, where my to-do list is done and I can be at rest." I'm not always aware of it, but at these moments, I am really longing for heaven.

The promise of the joys of heaven is one of the reasons I want to embrace and live by the truths I've shared in this book. They help us stay on the narrow road that leads straight to our real home. And when we arrive, we will be more than thankful for the true and right path because it led us to a glorious eternal life with the Lord in heaven. The problem is remembering that the best is yet to come when we are in the midst of the valleys.

Penny and her husband were missionaries for more than thirty years. They had recently returned to their home state and were excited about spending their remaining years near their children and grandchildren. Penny had faithfully served the Lord overseas, enduring the loss of a child, living in a challenging culture, and struggling with ongoing health concerns. She loved the Lord and was grateful for the life she had lived.

But the day we met, her heart was breaking. She wept because she had arrived home to family discord and separation. The hurt and betrayal were irreconcilable, and she was devastated. She grieved over the loss of a unified and close family. As a mature believer, Penny wasn't blaming God or even questioning why all this had happened. But she was overcome by her circumstances, and she needed someone to help bear her burden and remind her to keep an eternal perspective—that this life is only temporary. It will not always be like this—the best is yet to come.

When life overwhelms us, it's easy to focus on our immediate circumstances and forget the hope that heaven offers God's children. We live in a society consumed with trying to make our present life as pleasurable as possible because so many believe that what we experience here on earth is all there is. Often, we hear: "You only go around once." "This is as good as it gets." "Eat, drink, and be merry, for tomorrow we die."

We live wisely when we live with confidence and certainty that heaven is real and that the best is yet to come. It's wise to speak with assurance and anticipation of seeing Jesus and living in the place he has prepared for us. An integral part of the Good News is that this life on earth is not all there is; this life is momentary—only a "vapor" in light of eternity.[2] The promise that the best is yet to come comforts and compels us to endure during our brief stay on earth.

Many of the people whose stories are recorded in the Scriptures were able to persevere through difficult circumstances because they anticipated the joy of heaven. The writer of the book of Hebrews tells how Abraham followed God's path at great cost because he was "confidently looking forward to a city with eternal foundations, a city designed and built by God."[3]

Countless others were "tortured, refusing to turn from God in order to be set free. . . . Some were jeered at, and their backs were cut open with whips. Others were chained in prisons. Some died by stoning, some were sawed in half, and others were killed with the sword. Some went about wearing skins of sheep and goats, destitute and oppressed and mistreated."[4] How could they endure this suffering and still keep their faith? "They placed their hope in a better life after the resurrection."[5]

The common thread woven through the lives of these

men and women was their faith and expectant hope for the future. They considered themselves foreigners here on earth; they were just passing through on their way to eternity. The Scriptures remind us, "All these faithful ones died without receiving what God had promised them, but they saw it all from a distance and welcomed the promises of God. . . . They were looking for a better place, a heavenly homeland. That is why God is not ashamed to be called their God, for he has prepared a heavenly city for them."[6] They knew that what they suffered was nothing compared to the glory they would experience in heaven.

The defining quality of the people listed in Hebrews chapter 11 is their steadfast, persevering faith. They had given their lives to God and were willing to bring him glory, no matter what their circumstances might be. The apostle Peter wrote to encourage us to hold on to our faith in light of eternity: "There is wonderful joy ahead, even though you must endure many trials for a little while."[7]

Carol Kent, who is enduring the heartache of having her son in prison without the possibility of parole, has been able to maintain an eternal perspective. Carol has faithfully and honestly written about her journey through these devastating circumstances.

If I thought for a moment that there was no heaven, no end to my grief, no hope for my son's future, no end to sorrow, I would be tempted to "check out" right now. But Jesus' resurrection turns my personal

Good Friday into the hope of Easter Sunday, even if my joy is not fully realized in this life. . . .

. . . Hope's power is that we have the energy and desire to go on living because we believe something better is coming. That's the bottom line for the Christian: *Something more is coming.* There is more to this world than meets the eye. No matter what happens to you or your family, no matter what disappointments you encounter, no matter what diagnosis the doctor gives you, even if the end result is physical death, there is still *something more.*[8]

The "something more" is heaven. This life is not all there is. This life is only preparation for the eternal life to come, and what we will experience staggers the imagination. God gave the apostle John a vision of heaven, and this is what John tells us:

Then I saw a new heaven and a new earth, for the old heaven and the old earth had disappeared. . . . And I saw the holy city, the new Jerusalem, coming down from God out of heaven like a bride beautifully dressed for her husband.

I heard a loud shout from the throne, saying, "Look, God's home is now among his people! He will live with them, and they will be his people. God himself will be with them. He will wipe every tear from their eyes, and there will be no more death or sorrow or crying or pain. All these things are gone forever."[9]

At times, though, as we are on our way to the heavenly city, we can become fearful and hopeless. One day, Jesus asked his disciples to get in a boat and he said, "Let's cross to the other side of the lake."[10] While Jesus was sleeping in the boat, a fierce storm came up. High waves battered the boat, filling it with water. The disciples panicked and frantically woke the Lord, shouting at him, "Teacher, don't you care that we're going to drown?"[11] Jesus rebuked the wind and the water, and the storm immediately stopped. Then Jesus asked his disciples: "Why are you afraid? Do you still have no faith?"[12]

As I have thought about this incident, I realized that the one thing Jesus chided the disciples about was their lack of faith. He had made it clear that their destination was the other side of the lake. Getting there was a certainty. He was with them and at rest because he had said they were going to the opposite shore. What frightened and alarmed the disciples was encountering the storm as they made their way. They focused on their immediate situation and lost sight of the assurance of their ultimate destination.

In the midst of Nancy Guthrie's major "storm" of watching two babies die, she observed, "I have come to the place where I believe a yearning for heaven is one of the purposes and one of the privileges of suffering and of losing someone you love. I never had that yearning before, but I do now. You see, a piece of me is there. . . . I now see in a much fuller way that this life is just a shadow of our real life—of eternal life in the presence of God."[13]

Living in light of eternity enables us to grasp the fact that our lives here are only a miniscule part of God's plan. Understanding that the best is yet to come helps us to know that God is for us, not against us, and that we can trust him even when life doesn't make sense. No matter what our circumstances are, God is continually leading us in his true and right paths to the heavenly city.

Lisa Beamer, who lost her husband in the 9/11 tragedy, also understands that the certainty of heaven helps her persevere through her grief and loss:

> The tears still show up often in my life, sometimes when I least expect them. I know that even years from now, when the acute pain subsides, there will still be twinges of sadness because Todd's not here to enjoy life with us. But that's what life on this earth is—happiness mixed with sadness. True joy will never come here, but knowing it awaits me in eternity helps me progress through whatever life brings in the darkest of times. God has whispered two words to me over and over: *Look up. . . . Look up.* Through that quiet voice I'm reminded to look beyond my own little life to the Creator of the universe and what I know of his perspective. Without fail, looking up brings peace to my soul.[14]

Our friends Bruce and Rosie Das have kept looking up in spite of the loss of their only son, Eric, in the Gulf War. Eric was part of a select group of pilots who flew the first waves of combat missions into Iraq. At a memorial service we attended for him, his commander recounted Eric's last day on earth: "It was a Sunday, and Eric and his wife, who was also stationed in Iraq, went to chapel and had lunch together. Eric then took a nap and afterward was told that he would fly that evening. He was thrilled with this assignment and was eager to fly his mission. But over Tikrit, his jet went down under enemy fire. He died instantly and was immediately ushered into the presence of the Lord." The commander concluded, "That is what I would call a perfect day: He worshiped the Lord that morning, then met him face-to-face that evening."

In his Chronicles of Narnia series, C. S. Lewis confirms the wonders of being with the Lord. I had the pleasure of reading the Chronicles to our two oldest granddaughters, and I was blessed by the lovely word picture of heaven Lewis paints in *The Last Battle*. Peter, Lucy, Edmund, Jill, Eustace, and the others realize that they are in a new Narnia, heaven, and that they will never have to leave their beloved Aslan—the Christ figure. The regal lion Aslan says to them, "The term is over: the holidays have begun. The dream is ended: this is the morning."

Lewis concludes the book with this striking paragraph:

And as He spoke He no longer looked to them like a lion; but the things that began to happen after

that were so great and beautiful that I cannot write
them. And for us this is the end of all the stories,
and we can most truly say that they all lived happily
ever after. But for them it was only the beginning
of the real story. All their life in this world and all
their adventures in Narnia had only been the cover
and the title page: now at last they were beginning
Chapter One of the Great Story, which no one on
earth has read: which goes on forever: in which every
chapter is better than the one before.[15]

When we reach heaven, we will be home. The holidays
will start. It will be morning, and Chapter One of our eternity will begin.

The best will have come because we believed the truths of
Scripture and desired to live wisely.

*The Spirit of God whets our appetite by giving us a taste
of what's ahead. He puts a little of heaven in our hearts
so that we'll never settle for less. That's why we live with
such good cheer. You won't see us drooping our heads or
dragging our feet! Cramped conditions here don't get us
down. They only remind us of the spacious living conditions
ahead. It's what we trust in but don't yet see that keeps us
going. Do you suppose a few ruts in the road or rocks in
the path are going to stop us? When the time comes, we'll
be plenty ready to exchange exile for homecoming.*

2 CORINTHIANS 5:5-8, MSG

# A Prayer for Wisdom

Heavenly Father, thanks for whetting my appetite for heaven. How I need to keep an eternal perspective on my life. It's so easy for me to cling to and live for the temporal. It is so easy for me to lose hope when life is not lived on my terms and I begin to think that this life here on earth is all I have. May I remember that what I suffer here is nothing compared to the glory I will experience in heaven. Thank you for revealing yourself to me while I journey here. Thank you that you are always for me and that I can trust you in any circumstance. I am grateful for your presence with me now and the hope and joyful anticipation I have of seeing you face-to-face—for that, I cannot wait. Assuredly, the best is yet to come. In Jesus' name, amen.

# Reflections on the Truth

1. If you are not sure that you will spend eternity with Jesus, you can become certain right now. As you have read throughout this book, God loved the world so much that "He gave his one and only Son, so that everyone who

believes in him will not perish but have eternal life."[16] When you admit your need for a Savior and believe that Christ died for your sins, instead of perishing and experiencing eternal death, you will be born again to a new life in Christ. God loves you. He is aware of your sin and your failures, but through Christ's death on the cross, he has already paid the full price of your sin. If you confess your sin and accept his offer of forgiveness, you will become his child. And part of his inheritance to you is life with him—a full life now and eternal life with him in heaven. What an offer! If you want to become his child and experience the truth that the best is yet to come, write out a prayer of confession and surrender, telling God that you invite Christ into your life, that you accept his death on the cross as payment of your sin, and that you want to live wisely and travel his true and right paths until you reach the heavenly city.

2.   As you conclude this book, consider the truths you have read and the grand finale God has planned for you. Write a prayer thanking him for giving you life, for giving you his life to be lived in the world, and for the eternal life he has planned for you.

## Scripture to Believe

What we suffer now is nothing compared to the glory he will reveal to us later.

ROMANS 8:18

# Notes

AUTHOR'S NOTE
1. Proverbs 8:11.

INTRODUCTION: MY SEARCH FOR WISDOM
1. *Merriam-Webster's Collegiate Dictionary*, 11th ed. (2003), s.v. "existentialism."
2. Love: Matthew 5:44; Be reconciled: Matthew 5:23-24; Don't call attention: Matthew 6:1; Forgive: Colossians 3:13; Treasure: Matthew 6:21; Don't worry: Matthew 6:25-27; Stop judging: Matthew 7:1-5; Give: Luke 6:38; Humble yourself: James 4:10; Surrender: Matthew 10:39.
3. Matthew 7:13-14, PHILLIPS.
4. AMPC.

CHAPTER 1: MAYBE GOD IS RIGHT AFTER ALL
1. John 15:5.
2. Hosea 14:9, NLT-1996.
3. Jeremiah 9:23-24.
4. Psalm 24:1; see also 1 Chronicles 29:11.
5. Read the full story of Adam and Eve in Genesis 2 and 3.
6. Read the entire story of the Prodigal Son in Luke 15:11-32.
7. John 6:38, NLT-1996.
8. Hebrews 1:9, NLT-1996.
9. Matthew 18:15, NLT-1996.
10. Luke 6:28.
11. 1 Corinthians 13:4, NIV.
12. Psalm 25:8.

## CHAPTER 2: GOD IS FOR YOU, NOT AGAINST YOU

1. John 16:33.
2. Matthew 5:45.
3. John 11:5-6.
4. John 11:21-22.
5. Excerpt from newsletter written by Page Cvelich, May 31, 2000.
6. 1 John 4:9-10.
7. Oswald Chambers, *My Utmost for His Highest* (Westwood, N.J.: Barbour and Company, 1935), April 6.
8. Isaiah 53:5-6.
9. Isaiah 43:1-3.
10. Brian Birdwell and Mel Birdwell with Ginger Kolbaba, *Refined by Fire: A Family's Triumph of Love and Faith* (Carol Stream, IL: Tyndale, 2004), 205.
11. C. S. Lewis, in *Letters of C. S. Lewis*, quoted in *The Quotable Lewis*, ed. Wayne Martindale and Jerry Root (Carol Stream, IL: Tyndale, 1989), 408.
12. Isaiah 43:1-5.

## CHAPTER 3: TRUST GOD, EVEN WHEN IT DOESN'T MAKE SENSE

1. Read this incredible story and Nancy's study of the Old Testament book of Job in Nancy Guthrie, *Holding On to Hope* (Carol Stream, IL: Tyndale, 2004).
2. Guthrie, *Holding On to Hope*, 47.
3. 1 Peter 5:12, NLT-1996.
4. Elisabeth Elliot, *Suffering Is Not for Nothing*, audiotapes from *Gateway to Joy* (Lincoln, NE: Back to the Bible, 1999). Used by permission.
5. Elisabeth Elliot, *The Music of His Promises* (Ann Arbor, MI: Servant, 2000), 111.
6. Job 2:9.
7. Job 2:10, NLT-1996.
8. If you are not familiar with Moses, you can learn about him in the Old Testament book of Exodus.
9. Guthrie, *Holding On to Hope*, 46–47.
10. Carol Kent, *When I Lay My Isaac Down* (Colorado Springs, CO: NavPress, 2004), 13.
11. Lisa Beamer with Ken Abraham, *Let's Roll! Ordinary People, Extraordinary Courage* (Carol Stream, IL: Tyndale, 2002), 296, 276–77, 301.
12. Paula Rinehart, *Strong Women, Soft Hearts* (Nashville: Thomas Nelson, 2001), 81.

13. George Mueller, quoted in *Streams in the Desert*, comp. L. B. Cowman (Grand Rapids, MI: Zondervan, 1997), 36–37.
14. Psalm 73:25-26.

CHAPTER 4: FREEDOM FROM SELF IS A CHOICE
1. Robertson McQuilkin, *A Promise Kept* (Carol Stream, IL: Tyndale, 1998), 21–23.
2. Luke 9:23.
3. Luke 9:23, MSG.
4. John 8:31-32, 36, NLT-1996.
5. Ephesians 4:21-24, NLT-1996.
6. Galatians 2:20-21.
7. Luke 9:24-25, NLT-1996.
8. Esther 4:14, MSG.
9. Esther 4:16, NLT-1996.
10. To learn the whole story about Esther, read the Old Testament book of Esther.
11. Romans 14:7-9.
12. Luke 1:38, NLT-1996.
13. Luke 1:30, NLT-1996.

CHAPTER 5: KEEP YOUR HAND IN HIS
1. Oswald Chambers, *My Utmost for His Highest* (Westwood, N.J.: Barbour and Company, 1935), September 13.
2. Luke 10:40.
3. Luke 10:41-42.
4. Mark 4:19, NLT-1996.
5. Genesis 12:8, NLT-1996.
6. Chambers, *My Utmost for His Highest*, January 6.
7. BibleHub, "Genesis 12:8," accessed August 7, 2019, https://biblehub.com /parallel/genesis/12-8.htm.
8. Hebrews 4:12, NLT-1996.
9. John 15:7, NLT-1996.
10. W. Glyn Evans, *Daily with the King: 366 Daily Devotions* (Chicago: Moody, 1989), December 28.
11. NLT-1996.
12. Mark 4:18-19.

CHAPTER 6: GOD'S WORD IS ALL THE TRUTH YOU'LL EVER NEED
1. Psalm 34:22, KJV.
2. Amy Carmichael, quoted in Robert J. Morgan, *From This Verse* (Nashville: Nelson, 1998), March 6.

3. Proverbs 3:5-6, NRSV.
4. Proverbs 3:5-6, MSG.
5. 1 Corinthians 2:14, NLT-1996.
6. 2 Peter 1:20-21.
7. Ephesians 5:22.
8. John 17:17, NIV.
9. Wayne Grudem, *Systematic Theology: An Introduction to Biblical Doctrine* (Grand Rapids, MI: Zondervan, 1994), 83.
10. Ephesians 4:14-15, NLT-1996.
11. Hebrews 4:12, NLT-1996.
12. 1 Corinthians 6:18-20.
13. Story told by Erwin McManus at Sunset Presbyterian Church, July 13, 2003.
14. Gracia Burnham with Dean Merrill, *In the Presence of My Enemies* (Carol Stream, IL: Tyndale, 2004), 327–28.
15. Burnham, *In the Presence of My Enemies*, 328.
16. Birdwell and Birdwell, *Refined by Fire*, 150.
17. Philippians 4:6-7.
18. Matthew 7:24-27.

CHAPTER 7: YOU WILL NEVER REGRET DOING WHAT IS RIGHT

1. Luke 14:12-13, NLT-1996.
2. Henry Drummond, quoted in Corrie ten Boom, *Clippings from My Notebook* (Minneapolis, MN: World Wide Publications, 1982), 90.
3. Romans 6:23.
4. Ephesians 4:22-24, MSG.
5. Romans 6:12-13.
6. Genesis 39:6.
7. Genesis 39:9.
8. If you are not familiar with how Joseph's story ends, you can read the dramatic account in Genesis chapters 39 through 47.
9. G. K. Chesterton, quoted in *Quotes for the Journey, Wisdom for the Way*, comp. Gordon S. Jackson (Colorado Springs, CO: NavPress, 2000), 29.
10. Charles M. Sheldon, *In His Steps: "What Would Jesus Do?"* (Chicago: Advance Publishing, 1897).
11. 1 John 2:6.
12. Ephesians 4:24, MSG.
13. James 1:5, NLT-1996.
14. Psalm 34:15.
15. Isaiah 30:21, NIV.
16. This scripture is Psalm 119:5-6, MSG.

## CHAPTER 8: LOVE IS NOT OPTIONAL

1. Erma Bombeck, "Hot Tub Drowns Stress," *The Daily Register*, Thursday, February 26, 1981, http://www.digifind-it.com/redbank/_1980-1991 /1981/1981-02-26.pdf.
2. John 13:34.
3. Matthew 5:46, MSG.
4. *Merriam-Webster's Collegiate Dictionary*, 11th ed., s.v. "enemy."
5. Luke 6:27.
6. Romans 12:20-21, NLT-I.
7. Diane Reilly, quoted in Nancy Cobb and Connie Grigsby, *The Best Thing I Ever Did for My Marriage* (Sisters, OR: Multnomah, 2003), 79–80.
8. Reilly, quoted in Cobb and Grisby, *The Best Thing*, 81.
9. Hosea 1:2.
10. Hosea 3:1.
11. Romans 5:5.
12. 1 John 4:9-11.
13. Reilly, quoted in Cobb and Grigsby, *The Best Thing*, 81.

## CHAPTER 9: FORGIVENESS FREES THE FORGIVER

1. ten Boom, *Clippings from My Notebook*, foreword.
2. Pam Rosewell Moore, *Life Lessons from The Hiding Place: Discovering the Heart of Corrie ten Boom* (Grand Rapids, MI; Chosen Books, 2005), 145.
3. This story is based on Robert J. Morgan, *From This Verse* (Nashville: Nelson, 1998), December 22.
4. Luke 6:27-28, 37.
5. Romans 12:19. Emphasis added.
6. Matthew 6:12.
7. This story and the quotations are taken from Lisa Collier Cool, "The Power of Forgiving," *Reader's Digest*, May 2004, 93.
8. Proverbs 14:30, AMPC.
9. Ephesians 4:31-32.
10. Matthew 6:12.
11. Matthew 6:14-15.
12. Rinehart, *Strong Women, Soft Hearts*, 117.
13. Birdwell and Birdwell, *Refined by Fire*, 211.
14. Job 42:8.
15. Job 42:10.

16. W. F. Adeney, "The Accusers Accused," BibleHub, accessed August 8, 2019, https://biblehub.com/sermons/auth/adeney/the_accusers_accused .htm.

17. Nancy Guthrie, *Holding On to Hope*, 68–69.

18. Matthew 6:12.

19. John 8:4-5, NLT-1996.

20. John 8:7, NLT-1996.

21. John 8:11.

22. Genesis 50:20, NLT-1996.


CHAPTER 10: IT'S GOD'S LIFE

1. Burnham, *In the Presence of My Enemies*, 151–52, 153.

2. 1 Samuel 14:6-7, NLT-1996.

3. 2 Kings 5:3; you can read the entire story of Naaman's unusual experience of healing in 2 Kings 5:1-19.

4. Amos 7:14-15, NLT-1996.

5. Acts 9:36.

6. Romans 12:1.

7. Chambers, *My Utmost for His Highest*, February 24.

8. John 15:8, NLT-1996.

9. 1 Corinthians 10:31, NLT-1996.

10. A. W. Tozer, *The Pursuit of God: The Human Thirst for the Divine* (Camp Hill, PA: Christian Publications, 1993), 118.

11. John Ortberg, *The Life You've Always Wanted: Spiritual Disciplines for Ordinary People* (Grand Rapids, MI: Zondervan, 2002), 53–54.

12. Psalm 103:1-2.

13. Tozer, *The Pursuit of God*, 64.


A FINAL WORD: THE BEST IS YET TO COME

1. Psalm 55:6, NLT-1996.

2. James 4:14, NASB.

3. Hebrews 11:10.

4. Hebrews 11:35-37.

5. Hebrews 11:35.

6. Hebrews 11:13, 16, NLT-1996.

7. 1 Peter 1:6.

8. Kent, *When I Lay My Isaac Down*, 150, 108.

9. Revelation 21:1-4.

10. Mark 4:35.

11. Mark 4:38.

12. Mark 4:40.
13. Nancy Guthrie, *Holding On to Hope*, 57–58.
14. Beamer, *Let's Roll!*, 297.
15. C. S. Lewis, *The Last Battle,* The Chronicles of Narnia (New York: HarperCollins, 1956), 210–11.
16. John 3:16.

# About the Author

CYNTHIA HEALD uses her speaking engagements, Bible studies, and books to encourage women around the world to deepen their relationship with God. In addition to her popular Becoming a Woman of . . . Bible study series, which includes the bestselling *Becoming a Woman of Excellence* and *Becoming a Woman of Freedom*, Cynthia has also written *Loving Your Husband* and *Abiding in Christ: Becoming a Woman Who Walks with God*, a Gold Medallion–winning devotional. Her husband, Jack, joined her in writing an additional Bible study about marriage: *Loving Your Wife*. Cynthia's other nonfiction books include *Drawing Near to the Heart of God*, *Uncommon Beauty*, and *Life Promises for Women*.

When she is not writing or speaking, Cynthia loves to spend time with Jack and their four children and twelve grandchildren. She is an avid reader, especially of the classics. Cynthia enjoys taking bubble baths, having tea parties, and eating out.

Cynthia and Jack are full-time Navigator staff members in Tucson, Arizona.

# THE BEST GIFTS ARE FOUND ALONG THE FAITHFUL WAY

In *The Faithful Way*, beloved Bible study teacher Cynthia Heald challenges us to remain faithful wherever we are in our walk. This 31-day devotional will equip you to say, "I have remained faithful" as you learn to live intentionally to bring honor to Christ. Packed with Scripture, reflections, and short prayers on God's perfect love, living wisely, grace, forgiveness, accepting correction, being watchful, abiding in the Word, and much more, *The Faithful Way* will inspire and encourage both you and your friends.

**"Get ready for a month of motivation and encouragement!
I highly recommend Cynthia Heald's new book."**
- Linda Dillow, author of *Calm My Anxious Heart* and *Satisfy My Thirsty Soul.*

# THE NAVIGATORS® STORY

THANK YOU for picking up this NavPress book! I hope it has been a blessing to you.

NavPress is a ministry of The Navigators. The Navigators began in the 1930s, when a young California lumberyard worker named Dawson Trotman was impacted by basic discipleship principles and felt called to teach those principles to others. He saw this mission as an echo of 2 Timothy 2:2: "And the things you have heard me say in the presence of many witnesses entrust to reliable people who will also be qualified to teach others" (NIV).

In 1933, Trotman and his friends began discipling members of the US Navy. By the end of World War II, thousands of men on ships and bases around the world were learning the principles of spiritual multiplication by the intentional, person-to-person teaching of God's Word.

After World War II, The Navigators expanded its relational ministry to include college campuses; local churches; the Glen Eyrie Conference Center and Eagle Lake Camps in Colorado Springs, Colorado; and neighborhood and citywide initiatives across the country and around the world.

Today, with more than 2,600 US staff members—and local ministries in more than 100 countries—The Navigators continues the transformational process of making disciples who make more disciples, advancing the Kingdom of God in a world that desperately needs the hope and salvation of Jesus Christ and the encouragement to grow deeper in relationship with Him.

---

NAVPRESS was created in 1975 to advance the calling of The Navigators by bringing biblically rooted and culturally relevant products to people who want to know and love Christ more deeply. In January 2014, NavPress entered an alliance with Tyndale House Publishers to strengthen and better position our rich content for the future. Through *THE MESSAGE* Bible and other resources, NavPress seeks to bring positive spiritual movement to people's lives.

---

*If you're interested in learning more or becoming involved with The Navigators, go to www.navigators.org. For more discipleship content from The Navigators and NavPress authors, visit www.thedisciplemaker.org. May God bless you in your walk with Him!*

*Sincerely,*

DON PAPE
VP/PUBLISHER, NAVPRESS

*www.navpress.com*

CP1308